370 · 113

DERBY COLLEGE
LIBRARY

* D C 3 2 2 2 4 *

KU-634-472

WITHDRAWN
FROM STOCK

Planning and Implementing Your NVQ System

DERBY COLLEGE : WILMORTON
LIBRARY

Planning and Implementing Your NVQ System

Shirley Fletcher

KOGAN PAGE

London • Stirling (USA)

MACKWORTH COLLEGE
DERBY
LIBRARY

DATE. 27.11.02

ACC. No. 047124   DC32224

DERBY TERTIARY COLLEGE
WILMORTON LIBRARY
DATE: 28/5/98
ACC. No: 047124

First published in 1997

Apart from any fair dealing for the purposes of research or private study, or criticism or review, as permitted under the Copyright, Designs and Patents Act 1988, this publication may only be reproduced, stored or transmitted, in any form or by any means, with the prior permission in writing of the publishers, or in the case of reprographic reproduction in accordance with the terms of licences issued by the Copyright Licensing Agency. Enquiries concerning reproduction outside those terms should be sent to the publishers at the undermentioned address:

Kogan Page Limited
120 Pentonville Road
London N1 9JN
and
22883 Quicksilver Drive
Stirling, VA 20166, USA

© Shirley Fletcher, 1997

British Library Cataloguing in Publication Data

A CIP record for this book is available from the British Library.

ISBN 0 7494 2198 3

Typeset by Northern Phototypesetting Co Ltd, Bolton
Printed and bound in Great Britain by Clays Ltd, St. Ives Plc

Contents

Preface

New competence-based standards and National Vocational Qualifications continue to be tested and introduced across all industries. This book aims to provide help to those undertaking their introduction.

For most companies, a detailed understanding of the technicalities of standards development will not be required. However, a brief review of technical details is provided to assist understanding of the key concepts and issues which underlie the new structure of standards and assessment. Readers interested in further technical information will find the reference section of assistance. Those who require guidance on specific questions should turn to the 'Quick Reference Guide' in the Help Menu (p. 132).

Part I provides employers and managers with a strategic overview of recent developments in the field of competence-based provision, with specific emphasis on the potential benefits and challenges that these developments present for companies in the UK. Key questions and checklists to aid decision-making are included. Part I will also be of interest to senior training staff and to personnel professionals who need to know more about the purpose, structure and resource implications of implementing recent actions for change.

Part II takes training practitioners, and those with responsibility for 'hands on' implementation of change, step by step through the introduction of NVQs and the various uses of competence-based standards. The final chapters provide a brief overview and general guidance on how to make the best use of new competence-based developments within your company.

Checklists and charts provide user-friendly reference documents.

This book contains new case studies and information sections to outline the latest related developments within Training and Enterprise Councils, Investors in People, Assessor and Verifier Awards, and the 'Common Accord'.

Acknowledgements

I would like to thank all those who have contributed to this book. Some I have worked with closely in the past, others, not currently clients, kindly responded to a request for information.

I would particularly like to record my appreciation for the involvement of Martin Churcher of the Automobile Association and Barrie Oxtoby and Gary Ling of The UK Learning Organisations Network, who provided case studies.

Not to be forgotten are the many people who have worked hard on their NVQs in various projects with organisations such as Sony, Johnson & Johnson, Whitmans Laboratories, Marks & Spencer, Mazda and many small firms. The experiences of these people, and their in-house project managers, have all contributed to the development of new ideas for implementation.

Part I

The Company Perspective: Understanding the System

Introduction

- What are NVQs?
- What are standards of occupational competence?
- Why should my company introduce them?
- What are the resource implications?
- How do we get these standards?
- What do we do with them when we have them?
- Why do we have to change from the old system of standards and qualifications?

These are just some of the questions currently being asked by employers, managers and trainers across all industries in the UK. Many more such questions are listed in the Quick Reference Guide on page 132, along with the sections where readers will find the answers. But for many people, perhaps the biggest question is why these changes are taking place at all.

BACKDROP TO DEVELOPMENTS

During the 1980s a clear picture emerged in the UK – reports outlined imminent demographic changes, an unstable employment market, a 'skills gap' and a lack of economic competitiveness with our European neighbours. It became apparent that the UK vocational education and training (VET) system was unable to meet the demand for the skilled workforce that employers needed.

In 1981, the then Manpower Services Commission (MSC) produced its *New Training Initiative: An Agenda for Action* (MSC 1981). The key theme of this document was the clearly identified need for Britain to develop a 'flexible, adaptable workforce to cope with the uncertainties

that cloud the future'. It suggested that there were two crucial components to this development:

- a comprehensive training strategy
- standards of a new kind.

The new strategy became the three NTI objectives:

- develop skills training
- equip all young people for work
- widen opportunities for adults.

One of the most important aspects of this overall strategy, however, lies
in one simple phrase: 'at the heart of the initiative lie standards of a new
kind' (MSC 1981).

The new strategy depended upon these new standards becoming
available. However, initially, there was confusion about the concept.
Didn't we already have standards? What about British Standards? Did
the document mean 'training standards' or 'standards required in the
workplace'?

COMPETENCE, STANDARDS AND QUALIFICATIONS

Before long, the idea of a 'new kind of standard' became linked to the
term 'competence'. The idea of a 'flexible and adaptable workforce' was
superseded by that of a 'competent' one as reports such as *A Challenge to
Complacency* (Coopers and Lybrand 1985) and *Competence and Competition* (NEDC/MSC 1984) created an impact in the training world.

In 1986, the government published a White Paper, *Working Together,
Education and Training* (HMSO 1986) which set out plans for a radical
review of the UK education and training system. As the title of the paper
suggests, a key focus was greater partnership between the providers and
users of both education and training. One of the paper's key objectives
was to ensure that 'competence and achievement are recognised and
rewarded'. It stated that 'arrangements for standard setting and assessment also need improvement' and proposed that 'the structure of vocational qualifications be reformed'.

A report produced earlier that year, *Review of Vocational Qualifications
in England and Wales* (MSC/NEDC 1986), had suggested that the existing system of vocational qualifications lacked a clear, readily understandable pattern of provision while suffering from considerable overlap

and gaps in provision. It also suggested that there were many barriers to access to qualifications and inadequate arrangements for progression and/or transfer of credit. Finally, it suggested that assessment methods tended to be biased towards testing of knowledge rather than skill or competence, when what was needed by employers was application of skills and knowledge.

The report suggested that a vocational qualification should be defined as:

> a statement of competence, clearly relevant to work and intended to facilitate entry into, or progression in, employment, further education and training, issued by a recognised body to an individual.

It also suggested that this statement of competence should incorporate assessment of:

- skills to specified standards
- relevant knowledge and understanding
- the ability to use skills and to apply knowledge, and
- understanding the performance of relevant tasks.

The government White Paper took all these recommendations forward and solidly agreed that 'vocational qualifications need to relate more directly and clearly to competence required (and acquired) in work'. The radical reform of vocational qualifications therefore became a priority development area.

WHAT ARE THE BENEFITS?

The basic assumptions on which the new system of standards and qualifications operates are that training and work performance can be improved if people know exactly what is expected of them *within the working role*, and if they can be assessed reliably against those standards. In addition, if the expectations are defined by industry itself as explicit standards, and are agreed across industry, then recruitment, selection, and maintenance of high standards across the UK can also be improved.

As many companies have found, the key benefits of the new system include increased flexibility of training, an improvement in the identification of training needs and involvement of all staff at all levels in the overall performance (and therefore profitability) of the company.

More and more organisations are using the framework of competence-based standards as an HR tool – with NVQs becoming just one outcome of this flexible system. New competence frameworks encompass both national and organisational competences; or are developed as a synthesis of occupational and behavioural competences/ies.

This is not to say, of course, that the new system is a cure-all for economic problems at either macro or micro level; nor is it a five-minute wonder in terms of the investment required to implement it.

If your company is considering introducing competence-based standards and NVQs, this introduction must be planned, and staff must be trained in their operation. The case studies provided by companies who have begun this work illustrate the importance of these two aspects of change.

MYTHS AND MISCONCEPTIONS

Two main myths/misconceptions hamper understanding of the new structure of standards and qualifications.

NVQs are not training programmes

Many people perceive the new form of qualifications (NVQs, and SVQs in Scotland) as specified training programmes. The 'unit-based structure' of NVQs/SVQs becomes confused with 'modular training programmes'. The point will be clearly made throughout this book that NVQs are not training programmes. A unit of competence is a unit of *assessment* – it contains explicit standards of workplace performance.

NVQs are not awarded by the NCVQ

A second misconception is that the National Council for Vocational Qualifications (NCVQ) is the awarding body for this new form of certificate. NCVQ is *not* an awarding body, it is an *accrediting body*. NVQs are awarded by traditional bodies, such as City & Guilds, RSA, BTEC in England and Wales; SVQs are awarded by Scotvec in Scotland. In addition, some Industry Lead Bodies have become joint awarding bodies. NCVQ puts its stamp of approval on those qualifications which meet its criteria.

Of course other misunderstandings also occur. These are dealt with in the relevant sections of this book. The reader will find the Quick Reference Guide (p. 132) of help in locating answers to particular questions.

—— 1 ——

Actions to Change the UK System

1.1 NEW STANDARDS

Following publication of the government White Paper *Working Together, Education and Training* (HMSO 1986), action to introduce a new kind of standard and new forms of vocational qualifications was taken. The government directed the Manpower Services Commission (MSC, now the Department for Education and Employment) to:

> put in place dependable arrangements for setting standards of occupational competence across all sectors of industry.

It was agreed that these new standards should be defined *by industry* – a dramatic change from traditional forms of standard-setting – and should address questions such as the following:

- Who are the gatekeepers of standards for occupational performance of your workforce?
- Where are these standards?
- Are they accessible to all staff?
- Are they explicit?
- Do they represent expectations of performance or do they reflect what people need to know?

You might consider what your own answers to these questions would be. Traditionally, standards were embedded in curricula: they represented the *inputs* of training – what people had to learn. Assessment has in the past been biased towards testing of knowledge. Here was a shift to standards, and to associated assessment systems, which were to specify and assess *outputs* – what people had to *achieve*.

It is employers who recruit and employ staff, and it is employers who have expectations of the performance of those staff. It follows that employers and industry representatives should set the standards.

1.2 THE STANDARDS PROGRAMME

In order to achieve this, the MSC contacted all remaining Industrial Training Boards (ITBs) and Non-Statutory Training Organisations (NSTOs) and, through a series of conferences organised by the 'Industry Lead Body' (see below) and new 'Occupational Standards Branches' of MSC's head office, put into action a programme of development.

ITBs and NSTOs, as the bodies with responsibility for training within all sectors of industry, were each asked to supply an action plan to provide the following detail:

■ occupations for which each ITB/NSTO had training responsibility
■ a timescale for the development of standards of occupational competence for each occupation
■ a timescale for the development of new NVQs for each occupation
■ an estimated cost of development.

This information enabled the MSC to prepare an 'occupational map' in an attempt to ensure that all occupations across all sectors of all industries would achieve the development of new standards and NVQs.

Where ITBs and NSTOs did not exist (for example in the care sector), a long process of negotiation with a wide range of sectoral organisations began. Representatives from all areas of sectoral activity were brought together and a new kind of organisation – the Industry Lead Body – was formed.

1.3 INDUSTRY LEAD BODIES

Industry Lead Bodies (ILBs) are still being established across all sectors of industry and commerce. Their key responsibilities are the development of industry-defined standards of occupational competence and approval of a framework of new NVQs.

All new NVQs developed by industry need approval of the ILB before they can be submitted to the National Council for Vocational Qualifications (NCVQ) for final approval.

Funding for the development of standards and NVQs was provided in part by government. The MSC contributed up to 50 per cent of development costs and provided project managers from The Occupational Standards Branch. The remaining 50 per cent of costs had to be provided by the industry, usually in the form of staff time, accommodation for meetings and workshops, overheads, and so on.

In 1993, NCVQ began the establishment of Occupational Standards Councils – a further grouping of ILBs. These bodies now manage the development and updating of NVQs across industry sectors.

1.4 THE NATIONAL COUNCIL FOR VOCATIONAL QUALIFICATIONS (NCVQ)

Established in 1986, it was to be responsible for

bringing vocational qualifications in England and Wales into a new national framework to be called the National Vocational Qualification (NVQ). (MSC/NEDC 1981)

Initially the new framework was to consist of four levels, based on the following descriptions of standards of achievement:

Level 1
Occupational competence in performing a range of tasks under supervision.

Level 2
Occupational competence in performing a wider, more demanding range of tasks with limited supervision.

Level 3
Occupational competence required for satisfactory responsible performance in a defined occupation or range of jobs.

Level 4
Competence to design and specify defined tasks, products and processes and to accept responsibility for the work of others.

Expansion to level 4+ was to be discussed and the first developments to be undertaken in this area began in 1989, following long discussion and negotiation with the 250 professional bodies. In 1993, agreement was reached that development would not go beyond level 5.

The role of the NCVQ

The government set nine specific tasks for the NCVQ:

- Identify and bring about the changes necessary to achieve the specification and implementation of standards of occupational competence to meet the needs of the full range of employment, including the needs of the self-employed
- Design, monitor and adapt as necessary the new NVQ framework
- Secure the implementation of that framework by accrediting the provision of approved certifying bodies
- Secure comprehensive provision of vocational qualifications by the certifying bodies
- Secure arrangements for quality assurance
- Maintain effective liaison with those bodies having responsibilities for qualifications which give entry to, and progression within and from, the system of vocational qualifications into higher education and the higher levels of professional qualifications
- Collect, analyse and make available information on vocational qualifications and secure the operation of an effective, comprehensive and dependable database
- Undertake or arrange to be undertaken research and development where necessary to discharge these functions
- Promote the interests of vocational education and training and, in particular, of vocational qualifications and disseminate good practice.

The NCVQ and existing examining and validating bodies

The NCVQ (and Scotvec in Scotland) has a new and unique role. It is not an *examining* body – it does not set standards or assess examination papers centrally. Neither is it a *validating* body – it does not approve centres to operate training or learning programmes which lead to the award of a qualification.

In order to understand the NCVQ's role, it is essential to grasp one key point:

NVQs are not training or learning programmes.

The purpose of NVQ *assessment* is *certification* to national standards.

The key is *assessment of performance*. How people learn, what training programme they undertake or what method of training or learning is employed is, in effect, irrelevant. To achieve an NVQ, an individual must *demonstrate competent performance*.

The NCVQ's role, therefore, is not the same as an existing examining or validating body. Its remit is to develop policy for the vocational qualifications system as a whole, to negotiate to achieve the stated objectives from the system and to accredit qualifications of bodies offering awards within the national qualification framework. The NCVQ, therefore, is an endorsing or accrediting body. It approves qualifications which meet its criteria.

Scotland

The sole awarding body in Scotland is Scotvec, and it has been involved in all developments in England and Wales. The NCVQ's remit does not extend to Scotland, but new Scottish Vocational Qualifications (SVQs) operate in conjunction with ILBs in the same way as those south of the border.

1.5 IMPLICATIONS FOR EMPLOYERS

The forces and actions for change which have briefly been explored in this chapter present new challenges and benefits for employers. First, employers have been provided with an opportunity to directly influence the establishment of agreed standards of performance across all industries. Through representation on, and consultation with, ILBs, employers have been able to state exactly what they expect their workforce to do in each occupational role.

Second, this direct involvement in standard-setting has required employer investment – the standard-setting process takes considerable time and requires commitment to the overall concepts and objectives of the standards programme.

Third, a focus on performance in the workplace requires new forms of assessment of performance. Performance can be assessed most effectively *in the workplace*. Employers therefore have to consider how such workplace assessment systems will operate.

A fourth issue is that development and implementation of new standards and qualifications require a change in attitude. Employers and their staff become much more involved in the individual development process. Assessment of performance in the workplace provides a solid foundation for training-needs analysis and more effective targeting of training. In the last decade, many reports have demonstrated that Britain is nowhere near the top of the list when it comes to investing in training and development of staff.

If employers are to reap the benefits of new standards which specify performance, which require workplace assessment, which lead to national recognition of competent performance, should they not also be investing more in well-targeted training and development?

Last but by no means least is the issue of cost. These changes require an investment in development and a further investment in implementation. A key issue to be considered by users of new systems of competence-based standards and qualifications is one of return on investment. What are the benefits of these new standards and qualifications? Help with this issue is provided in the following chapters.

DERBY COLLEGE : WILMORTON LIBRARY

—— 2 ——

The New Structure of Qualifications

2.1 WHAT IS MEANT BY COMPETENCE?

New occupational standards are based on a concept of competence which emerged through long debate. The theoretical discussions regarding a precise definition are adequately covered in a wide range of technical papers. What is of key interest to employers is the applicability of the concept to the real-life employment arena.

The simplest definition of the new concept of competence is:

the ability to perform activities within an occupation.

However, this says nothing about how well the activities have to be performed! The gradual emergence of a more explicit definition occurred as attempts to define clear and meaningful standards continued:

competence is a wide concept which embodies the ability to transfer skills and knowledge to new situations within the occupational area. It encompasses organisation and planning of work, innovation and coping with non-routine activities. It includes those qualities of personal effectiveness that are required in the workplace to deal with co-workers, managers and customers. (Training Agency 1988/89)

This broad, if lengthy, definition attempts to cover all aspects of 'competent' performance in a realistic working environment.

2.2 WHAT EXACTLY ARE NVQs?

The formal definition of a National Vocational Qualification is that it is
'a statement of competence' which incorporates specified standards in
'the ability to perform in a range of work-related activities, the skills,
knowledge and understanding which underpin such performance in
employment' (Training Agency 1988/89).

Each NVQ covers a particular area of work, at a specific level of
achievement and fits into the NVQ framework.

The NVQ framework

The initial NVQ framework had four levels; now level 5 is the highest
and ultimate classification. The levels indicate competence achieved.

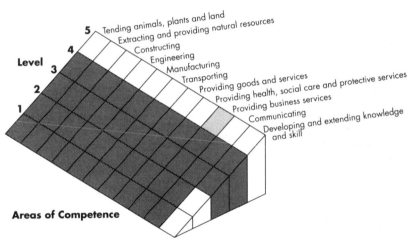

Figure 2.1 Example of NVQ levels of competence

'Areas of work' refer to occupations such as engineering, catering,
agriculture and so on. Various reports on 'occupational mapping' have
been carried out in recent years, the most widely known being TOC
(training occupations classification). The NCVQ has reviewed the various classifications and also the information provided by ILBs as part of
its 'mapping exercise' for standards development. This review has led to
a categorisation of occupations that forms the basis of the NCVQ database of standards and qualifications.

What do NVQs look like?

The unit-based structure of NVQs provides a hierarchical model of qualifications with standards forming the foundation stones.

As we have noted, the NVQ itself is a statement of competence which can be achieved through accumulation of 'credit' in the form of units of competence. Each unit is made up of defined standards of competence. The structure of an NVQ can therefore be illustrated as in Figure 2.2. Following publication of the Beaumont Report (Beaumont 1996), an increasing emphasis on 'evidence requirements' will be apparent. This aims to ensure that the quality of assessment is maintained, with a focus on 'performance evidence' (see Chapter 4 for further guidance).

Progression through the NVQ framework can be seen as an incremental development. Increments will take different forms in different occupational areas. This is because individuals are able to increase their competence in a number of ways:

- By increasing the range of work-related activities they are able to perform
- By mastering more complex work-related activities
- By specialisation.

Individuals may not necessarily progress through the framework in a straightforward vertical order – some lateral progression, across related sectors, is perfectly feasible. For example, there is a great deal of overlap between sectors such as retail and the travel industry. It is quite possible that an individual who has achieved a level 2 qualification in retail, through assessment during work as a retail assistant in a general department store, might progress to a level 3 qualification in travel services through further assessment while in employment within the travel agency department of the same store. This same individual may continue to develop a career in travel services, or may move on in retail management. Either route is possible and qualifications achieved will have relevance in both sectors.

This dual relevance, or 'cross-sectoral applicability', is made possible by a further aspect of the NVQ structure – its *unit basis*, which facilitates credit accumulation.

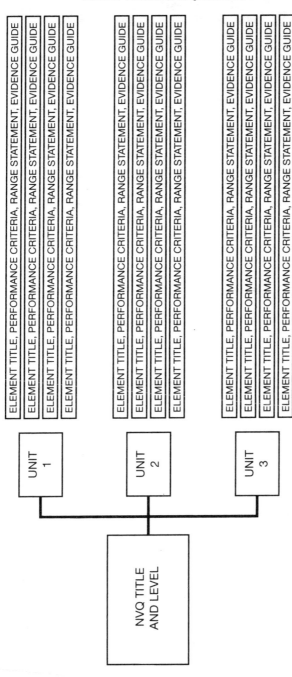

Figure 2.2 NVQ structure

2.3 NVQs AND TRADITIONAL QUALIFICATIONS

A key aim of the NCVQ's work is that open access to both the acquisition and accreditation of competence should be made available to as many individuals as possible. In addition, the access system must provide flexibility: modes, locations, entry requirements and timescales of learning should not restrict such access.

As noted in Chapter 1, traditional qualifications are tied to a specific course of study and require a set time commitment and set assessment methods, usually involving study at a specified centre. There are also often conditions of entry to study, such as age limits or previously acquired qualifications.

Qualifications are traditionally, therefore, only available if an individual is able to overcome certain barriers to or restrictions on access.

2.4 CREDIT ACCUMULATION

Traditional qualification barriers to access include:

- age
- time-based study
- location of study
- specified course of study
- specified assessment methods.

Traditional qualifications are awarded 'en bloc' – individuals obtain the whole qualification or nothing at all. As new NVQs operate on a credit accumulation basis, each qualification is comprised of a number of units of competence, and each unit is independently achievable and separately certificated (see Figure 2.3). Individuals are therefore able to achieve a full qualification by achieving *one unit at a time*. Units can be collected over time, each unit being assessed in the workplace and therefore relating directly to the individual's current work role.

While traditional routes of study (and routes to qualifications) will still be available, and indeed encouraged, the introduction of NVQs means that this traditional mode of accreditation will no longer be the only means available. Widening of access to assessment, removal of time-based study and the introduction of assessment in the workplace have removed restrictions which prevented a wide range of individuals from achieving formal recognition for their skills.

Figure 2.3 Unit-based structure

NVQs are not linked to any specified course of study, nor are they time-based; candidates achieve units at their own pace, the primary form of assessment is observation of performance in the workplace and there are no restrictions of age, previous qualifications etc, regarding access to assessment.

2.5 WHO AWARDS NVQs?

The NCVQ is not an awarding body, it is an accrediting body. It there-fore approves qualifications which meet its published criteria (see Part III). The NCVQ covers only England and Wales; in Scotland, Scottish Vocational Qualifications (SVQs) are awarded by Scotvec (the sole awarding body in Scotland) which has agreed to work with the NCVQ to ensure commonality of standards in the UK.

The traditional awarding bodies – City & Guilds, RSA, BTEC, Scotvec, ITD, professional bodies and so on – still award national qual-ifications. They also submit those qualifications which meet the NCVQ's criteria to the NCVQ for approval as an NVQ. (BTEC now operates in a joint arrangement as EdExcel.)

Awarding bodies have been involved in the development of national standards and have reviewed and restructured their own awards as a result of the changes that have been taking place. As the key to NVQs is assessment, the modes and methods of assessment used by awarding bodies have also been reviewed. Assessment of actual performance in the workplace necessitates change in the role of awarding body assessors and moderators. Credit accumulation requires a change in the structure of national qualifications. Competence-based standards defined by industry have to be used as the basis for all qualifications which are to be submitted to the NCVQ.

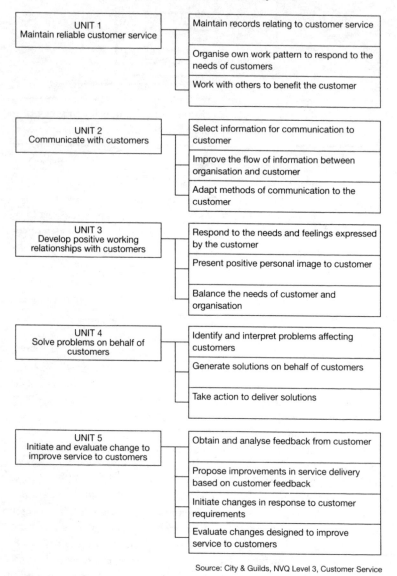

Source: City & Guilds, NVQ Level 3, Customer Service

Figure 2.4 Unit structure of an NVQ

Some ILBs have decided to work with existing validating and examining bodies to become 'joint awarding bodies'. For example, the Hotel and Catering Training Company is a joint awarding body with City & Guilds and BTEC for NVQs in their industry.

It is important to recognise that the NCVQ itself is *not* an awarding body. It approves qualifications which meet its criteria. Your employees will still, therefore, be certificated by a familiar examining or validating body, but if the particular qualification they achieve has been approved as an NVQ, the certificate will include the NCVQ seal of approval in addition to the awarding body's title.

An example certificate is shown in Figure 2.5.

2.6 WHO DEVELOPS NVQs – AND HOW?

Chapter 1 outlined the government directives which led to the then Manpower Services Commission's responsibility for the standards programme and to the establishment of the NCVQ. The same section also briefly reviewed the establishment of ILBs and Occupational Standards Councils and the arrangements for funding these bodies to undertake development of standards within their industry sectors.

While ILBs have overall responsibility for development of standards and NVQs within their sectors, the actual development must be undertaken *by industry itself*. Each ILB manages a project in which experts from the industry work with a technical consultant to define competence-based standards.

Once the standards are developed, they are circulated throughout the industry, often with a questionnaire, or in test-bed sites to ascertain whether they have real meaning for users and whether they actually reflect workplace practice.

The development of competence-based standards can be a lengthy process, particularly in large, complex sectors of industry where many organisations have interest in 'owning' the development process. Where no established ILB exists, one has to be set up. This can involve long negotiations with industry training organisations, employers associations, voluntary bodies, trade unions, professional bodies and so on.

The complexities of the standards development programme are illustrated in Table 2.1, which outlines the stages involved in reaching a final draft of competence-based standards for one sector of industry. This process also applies to the reviewing and updating of NVQs every three to five years.

National Vocational Qualification

This Certificate
is awarded to

**The holder has one or more formal Records of Achievements
by which this Certificate was earned**

Awarded

Director-General
City and Guilds of London Institute

Director of Training and Development
Hairdressing Training Board

The City and Guilds of London Institute is incorporated by Royal Charter and was founded in 1878

Figure 2.5 An NVQ certificate

Table 2.1 Designing competence-based standards

Action required

Identify gaps in NVQ framework – which industries do not yet have NVQs?

Identify/set up Industry Lead Body (ILB)

Agree ILB action plan

ILB completes occupational mapping to identify key work roles within its sector

Functional analysis to 'unit of competence' level completed by ILB with help of technical consultant

Standards of competence defined for each unit

Standards verified by industry through consultation process

Refinement of standards based on feedback from industry

Units of competence grouped to meet industry requirements (basis of industry's NVQ framework established)

In large sectors, the ILB will establish its own NVQ framework. This framework illustrates how the standards have been incorporated into NVQs at various levels (see the NVQ framework on p. 13), and would also demonstrate various progression routes.

Once testing of standards is complete, work continues on the development of an associated assessment system and procedures for maintenance of standards (quality control mechanisms).

Involvement of and negotiations with relevant awarding bodies are undertaken to establish quality control and certification procedures and, again, the assessment system is tested within the industry. This process is illustrated in Table 2.2.

When all consultation and negotiation are complete, the entire package of standards, assessment and certification is submitted to the NCVQ by the awarding bodies for approval.

Table 2.2 Designing competence-based assessment

Action required

Determine modes of assessment

Develop assessment procedures

Develop recording procedures

Test assessment model and procedures in industry

Refine assessment model and procedures as necessary

Design unit certificate and NVQ certificate

Negotiate quality control procedures with awarding body(ies)

Determine criteria for approval of assessment centres

Determine arrangements for approval of assessors

Links with related industry sectors will also be established and transfer of relevant credits (units of competence) between related sectors will be agreed.

The development process involves the use of a functional approach rather than an analysis of tasks or skills. By identifying the key functions, working top-down from sectoral to individual level, a broader view of work activity (and therefore competence) is obtained. This broad view of competence is represented in Figure 2.6.

In this way, the resulting standards do not simply reflect the basic tasks that individuals and organisations undertake, nor do they reflect 'jobs' (many of which can have the same title but differing content or vice versa). An emphasis on *functions* should lead to standards which provide a realistic and explicit definition of *work roles*. Examples of the standards developed in this way are given in the next chapter.

Tasks
Task management
Contingency management
Role/job environment

Figure 2.6 Components of competence (adapted from the Job
Competence Model, Mansfield and Mathews 1985)

2.7 IMPLICATIONS OF THE NEW STRUCTURE

These radical changes obviously have enormous implications for both
providers and users of vocational qualifications. Changes in the assessment process, the removal of mandatory links to specified training programmes, the removal of barriers to access and the abolition of
time-based study all lead to increased potential flexibility; they also
require fundamental changes in the approach to training, development
and assessment.

For *providers*, these changes mean that methods and modes of training
delivery must undergo complete review. Closer liaison between
providers and employers is required. New methods of delivery and a
complete revision of curriculum are needed if the qualification support
system is to operate on a credit-accumulation basis. Arrangements for
continuous assessment and for recording of achievement must also be
put in hand.

For *employers*, the potential is enormous for flexibility of training and
development provision, increased cooperation and involvement with
providers, better targeted training and performance assessment,
improved recruitment, selection, and manpower planning, and ulti-
mately, improved economic performance (see Fletcher 1993).

To achieve this potential, however, employers must be prepared to
invest in the establishment of work-based assessment systems and the
maintenance of quality standards of performance.

Companies are finding that the lead time for introducing competence-based standards and NVQs is longer than the original estimates.

Changing the system requires a complete plan for staff briefing and training of assessors as well as a possible review of all in-company training.

For *individuals*, guidance has to be provided on the availability and applicability of NVQs and the units of competence of which they are comprised. Once individuals have identified units of competence relevant to their particular needs, further guidance on suitable programmes of development and progression routes will also be required.

These implications, with their inherent challenges and benefits, are examined in more detail in the following chapters.

A New Kind of Standard

3. I A FOUNDATION FOR COMPETENCE

Chapter 1 began with a brief overview of challenges facing the UK and of the new strategy for meeting those challenges which was based on 'standards of a new kind'.

Currently, standards of performance are perhaps the major area of interest to employers. Standards reflect what actually happens in the workplace – and what happens in the workplace affects productivity and profitability. (Qualifications are important to employers for other reasons; the pros and cons of this issue are examined in the next chapter.)

Also in Chapter 1, you were asked to consider a number of questions relating to the standards currently in use in your own organisation. To refresh your memory, these questions were:

- Who are the gatekeepers of standards for occupational performance of your workforce?
- Where are these standards?
- Are they accessible to all staff?
- Are they explicit?
- Do they represent expectations of performance or do they reflect what people need to know?

For many years, there has been a general concern about Britain's performance in the economic market. This concern is manifest in the enormous interest in the introduction of in-company schemes relating to total quality and the accreditation of companies to meet ISO 9000 quality assurance.

This emphasis on quality relates directly to the performance of each individual employee.

When recruiting and selecting staff, no doubt you have some form of job and person specification from which to develop a profile of the sort of person you are looking for. For some employers, experience is a key issue; for others, qualifications are high on the priority list.

Many job descriptions and most of the UK vocational qualifications, as well as the education and training system, have not been based on *specification or achievement of precise standards*. As a result, industry has been disappointed in both the quality and actual performance of its recruited employees.

If, as is traditionally the case, standards are based on inputs or what has to be learned, and assessment is biased towards testing of what people know (as in course assignment and examination), it is not surprising to find that actual performance in job roles falls short of expectations and requirements.

However, if standards were based upon expectations of performance, set by industry, and linked to qualifications which could only be achieved through *actual demonstration of the required performance*, then quality of recruitment, selection and actual workplace activity should improve.

The development of nationally agreed standards of competence provides a benchmark for performance across all occupations, provided that industry is fully involved in the development and consultation processes. This was the basic philosophy behind national developments relating to standards (and NVQs). However, from the employers' view point, qualifications are not the main reason for having precise standards. A real test of this 'standard of a new kind' would be its applicability and utility across the spectrum of employment practices.

The issue of utility is addressed later in this chapter. First we need to consider what these new standards offer companies and to review exactly what form they take.

3.2 WHAT MAKES THE NEW STANDARDS DIFFERENT?

Two key aspects of the new competence-based standards make them completely different from those traditionally used in training, vocational assessment and the award of certificates. The first relates to the basic concept of *competent performance* and has already been outlined:

competence-based standards reflect **expectations** *of workplace performance;* *competence-based standards express* **outcomes** *of workplace activity.*

The second key aspect is one which offers considerable potential for future training, development and assessment plans. It is also one which many people fail to grasp – mainly because it requires a complete shift of thinking. Unlike traditional, curriculum-based (input) standards, which are linked to a specific training or learning programme (and also linked to predefined forms of assessment), new competence-based standards are *completely independent* of both training and assessment processes (see Figure 3.1).

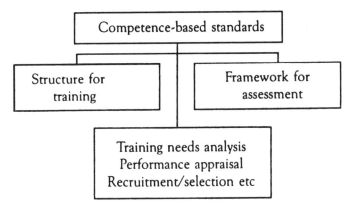

Figure 3.1 Independence of competence-based standards

Because the 'new kind of standard' is focused entirely on required performance (including the application of underpinning knowledge and understanding), it provides a foundation on which training programmes, and/or assessment processes can be developed.

3.3 WHAT DO THESE DIFFERENCES MEAN FOR MY COMPANY?

Discussions with a range of employers lead to one key answer to this question – *flexibility.*

As the new forms of standards are completely independent of training and/or assessment systems (although they are integral to assessment leading to NVQs), their potential use at organisational level is enormous. The last two sections of this chapter provide some stimulus for thought on this issue.

Organisations which have introduced competence-based standards have recognised the benefits of having explicit statements of performance available to all staff. Some of the benefits include:

- staff know exactly what is expected of them
- assessment to specified standards means training needs can be easily identified
- training can be targeted to real needs
- as standards are not linked to any particular training or learning programme, both in-company and external training can be used as well as a wide range of training methods.

3.4 STANDARDS AND NVQs

New NVQs use nationally agreed standards of competence as the framework for *assessment* of occupational competence.

One of the most difficult concepts for many individuals to grasp was outlined in Chapter 1:

NVQs are *not* training or learning programmes

If your company introduces NVQs, therefore, it is *not* introducing a new training programme, it is introducing a new form of *assessment* of occupational competence which leads to the award of an NVQ. Issues of competence-based assessment are outlined in Chapter 4.

The structure of an NVQ was illustrated in Chapter 2 (see p. 15). The foundation stones of all NVQs are competence-based standards, the basic composition of which is:

- element of competence
- performance criteria
- range statement
- evidence guide
- units of competence.

Elements of competence

An element of competence is a description of something which a person who works in a given occupational area should be able to do. It reflects action, behaviour or outcome which has real meaning in the occupational sector to which it relates. For example:

■ create, maintain and enhance effective working relationships (management competences)
■ inform customers about products and services on request (financial services competences).

The issue of being *outcome-based* is of prime importance. This represents a strong shift away from traditional standards which are based on inputs or curriculum (ie, what has to be learned).

Performance criteria

Performance criteria are statements by which an assessor judges the evidence that an individual can perform the workplace activity specified by the element of competence. In effect, the performance criteria enhance the element of competence by stating explicit measures of outcomes (see Figure 3.2).

Performance criteria consist of a short sentence with two components – a critical outcome and an evaluative statement (how the activity has resulted in the required result).

Range statement (and range indicators)

Range statements describe the contexts and limits within which performance to the identified standards is expected, if the individual is to be deemed competent.

Range indicators serve the same purpose but some words of caution are relevant. There are two reasons why range indicators rather than range statements may be found in published national standards:

■ Range indicators are often developed as the first attempt at defining more explicit range statements. The presence of 'range indicators' may, therefore, suggest that further development work is being undertaken at national level.
■ In 'generic' occupational areas (such as management or training, which operate across all industrial sectors), it may only be possible to develop range 'indicators'. As these generic standards will be used across a wide range of commercial and industrial sectors, flexibility in specifying the detailed range statement will be a paramount consideration.

UNIT TITLE:	A22 IDENTIFY INDIVIDUAL LEARNING NEEDS
ELEMENT TITLE:	A221 Identify available learning opportunities

PERFORMANCE CRITERIA

a Training and development opportunities available are clearly and accurately identified.

b Conditions and characteristics of training and development opportunities available are clearly and accurately identified.

c Where learners require more detailed information about learning programmes offered they are referred to the appropriate person.

d Resources available and organisational requirements for the delivery of training and development opportunities are accurately identified.

e Where learners require training and development which cannot be met by the organisation they are referred to appropriate alternative providers.

RANGE STATEMENTS

Training and development opportunities: methods, programmes, qualifications.

Condition and characteristics of learning programmes: entry conditions, time and place, mode of training methods used.

Resources: people, time, finance, materials, equipment, facilities.

PERFORMANCE EVIDENCE REQUIRED

A Identified training and development opportunities and their conditions and characteristics.
B Notes on resources and organisational requirements.

KNOWLEDGE EVIDENCE REQUIRED

i Conditions and characteristics of different training and development opportunities.
ii Training and development opportunities available.
iii Resources available.
iv Organisational requirements.
v Suitable alternative providers.

GUIDANCE TO ASSESSORS OF THIS ELEMENT

1. Performance evidence requirements relating to 'identifying training and development opportunities' the candidate should provide evidence of identifying learning opportunities for at least two individuals covering at least two different types of training and development opportunities.

Example of a national standard (*Source:* TDLB Standards 1992)

Figure 3.2 Example of a national standard
Source: TDLB Standards 1992

A range statement is a guide to an assessor. A judgement of 'competent' denotes that an individual is able to produce the desired outcomes within the requirements of their work role. This may mean that the individual is able to complete the same activity using a range of equipment or materials, or that they can complete a number of activities within a working context, or within a range of contexts.

If assessment of competence is to be realistic, competent performance in a range of equipment, materials and contexts must be assessed. This is where the range statement serves to 'set the scene' for assessment.

Evidence guide

An evidence guide (or specification) provides the assessor with an outline of requirements for assessment. The most up-to-date practice requires that all assessment includes 'performance evidence'. Simulations (eg, skills test) can only be used to supplement assessment (see Chapter 4).

Units of competence

When competence-based standards are developed, using the functional approach as described in Chapter 2, the initial analysis provides titles for *units of competence*.

These units of competence represent workplace activity which

- can be undertaken by one individual
- is worthy of separate certification (ie, as a 'credit' towards a full NVQ).

Units of competence *are not training modules*. As noted in Chapter 1, NVQs are not training or learning programmes. The components of a unit of competence will probably form the structure on which a training programme will be based, but a unit of competence reflects what has to be achieved in the workplace. It is expressed as an *output* of activity. No sequence of learning or learning input is specified – this is an issue for individual employers to determine when deciding on training needs.

What about knowledge?

This is a question frequently asked about the new competence-based standards – an understandable question when it appears that the focus is totally on performance in the workplace. Those of us who are familiar with assessment processes within traditional qualifications will be aware that there is a 'knowledge bias' within testing procedures.

A common complaint from employers in the past has been that 'qualified people', although recruited on the basis of having achieved a relevant qualification, still need considerable training because 'they know what to do but have little experience of actually doing it'. A valid concern about new forms of standards and qualifications, therefore, is that those who have been able to demonstrate *performance* will 'be able to do, but not understand what they do'!

The issue of the role of knowledge and understanding within competence-based standards was debated long and hard with all partners in the vocational education and training system. The original directive for 'standards of a new kind' and for the 'reform of vocational qualifications' stipulated that it was the 'application of skills and knowledge' that was of importance in competent performance.

Initial ideas implied that knowledge could be identified within competence-based standards as 'elements of competence' or 'performance criteria'. However, this proved not to be the case. This approach simply encouraged separate treatment of 'knowledge and understanding', whereas the aim was to provide an integrated expression of competent performance.

Through various exploratory projects it became clear that, in some respects, 'underpinning knowledge and understanding' could be *inferred* from performance (ie, the assessor, as a person experienced in the particular occupational field, would be able to make this inference).

A further issue relating to knowledge and understanding concerns the question of transfer of skills – application of knowledge means being able to transfer 'what you know and understand' within different contexts, or to the use of different equipment, or to dealing with contingencies. In this respect, the range statement acts as a guide (for the assessor) to ensure that related knowledge and understanding are assessed.

This section has provided a very brief overview of the technical issues involved in the development of competence-based standards. For those who wish to delve deeper into technical issues, relevant technical documents are listed in the reference section.

3.5 THE USES OF STANDARDS

Consider for a moment how your organisation currently uses standards – if you have them. We have already mentioned that recruitment and selection may utilise some kind of profile for both job and person. What about activities such as manpower planning, performance appraisal, training needs analysis, or judging the effectiveness of training provision?

How about actions for change? Do you refer to standards when considering introducing new technology, or implementing a plan for multi-skilling, or restructuring the organisation?

Then there is the question of 'to whom do standards relate?' Do you have standards only for skilled workers (maybe in some form of workshop manual)? Or do you have clear standards for all of your workforce, including management?

The big questions are:

- On what basis do you make decisions regarding the restructuring or reorganisation of your workforce?
- How do you take a 'skills audit' of your workforce?
- What information do you use when making decisions about the recruitment and selection of new staff?
- On what basis are decisions regarding future manpower planning made?
- How do you measure performance?

Perhaps an even bigger question is:

- **How do you define performance?**

We come back to attitudes. Does 'performance' immediately suggest issues at organisational level? Issues of profitability, productivity, competitive advantage in the market place? Or does 'performance' also suggest individual work activity which results in these higher level measures?

If the latter is true, then you are an employer who has at least considered the importance of the contribution of each member of your workforce to the overall 'performance' of your company. You may well have an appreciation of the key part that explicit, industry-defined standards could play in all employment activities.

Potential uses of explicit standards of performance for all work roles might include:

- identifying training needs within the context of organisational objectives
- designing training programmes
- identifying changes in roles
- planning multiskilling activities
- setting objectives for self-development
- improving performance appraisal systems
- manpower planning.

(See also Fletcher 1993.)

3.6 CONTEXTUALISING STANDARDS

Nationally agreed standards of occupational competence are, as noted at the beginning of this chapter, a benchmark for competence across a sector. In areas such as management, or training and development, or administrative and clerical work, national standards will be applicable across a wide range of sectors.

At organisation (ie, company) level, decisions to 'contextualise' standards may be taken. Some organisations may feel that the national standards need to be enhanced in order to reflect the company mission and objectives. Some may wish to incorporate specific company standards.

There is no reason why this cannot be done. If nationally agreed standards of occupational competence for relevant work roles remain as the basis of any assessment process leading to award of NVQs, then additional information can be added to these standards.

Many organisations may already have invested in development of 'company standards'. Again, these can either be revised to a competence-based format, or incorporated into those agreed by the sector. It is likely that companies will need consultancy support to complete this work.

Part II

Planning
Your
System

INTRODUCTION

One of the first things you must ask yourself when considering the introduction of NVQs is:

Why do we want to implement NVQs?

This may sound rather obvious, but it is often not given the consideration it needs.

The following chapters take you through the key planning issues. Further help is available in my other books which provide more specific help and examples (see the References section).

4

Key Questions for Decision-making

This chapter provides guidance and stimulus for thought for employers, managers and trainers who are considering the introduction of competence-based standards and NVQs. It assumes that readers are familiar with the key concepts and operational requirements of these new trends in assessment and certification.

To aid you in the decision-making process, key questions relating to the introduction of competence-based standards and new NVQs are provided in a hierarchical order. These questions are:

- Should we introduce standards and NVQs?
- How do we start?
- What needs to be done?
- How we will use standards throughout the company?

There are no model answers; each company will need to make its decisions based on:

- management understanding of the new structure of standards and NVQs
- the perceived benefits of implementation
- consideration of the key issues involved, including resource and cost implications.

The first of these requirements for decision-making can be achieved by reference to Chapters 1–3 of this book. Readers may wish to refer back to appropriate sections for clarification of specific points.

4.1 DOES MY COMPANY NEED COMPETENCE-BASED STANDARDS AND NVQs?

Potential benefits – competence-based standards

- Staff will know exactly what is expected of them in terms of outcomes of performance
- Assessment systems (including performance appraisal) can be used effectively to identify training needs
- Training delivery can be targeted to real needs, thus reducing downtime and increasing return of investment in training
- Standards are not linked to any one training/learning programme, so in-company and/or external training can be designed/provided on a completely flexible basis
- Standards will be accessible by all staff, so continuous assessment can be conducted
- Supervisors and line managers can all become involved in ongoing workplace assessment
- Training programmes can be designed using the standards as the basic design structure, thus making programmes relevant to work roles and more focused on learning which can be put into practice in the workplace
- Standards in competence-based format provide an objective way of looking at current and future manpower needs
- Standards can be used as a basis for recruitment specifications and structuring of interview questions
- Standards would provide consistency and quality and would contribute to the implementation and achievement of ISO 9000 and/or the introduction of total quality management (TQM).

Potential benefits – NVQs

- External recognition for employees
- Workplace assessment by in-company staff – all supervisors and first-line managers involved in day-to-day assessment of performance
- Meets requirements for operation of training credits and other government programmes in providing access to NVQs
- Company assessment and career planning can be linked to progressive structure of national qualifications

- Employees can achieve qualifications without having to attend lengthy periods of study
- Workplace assessment contributes to more effective identification of training needs
- Flexibility of training provision – the company can design its own training programmes, or use external providers who can provide training which is based on the specified standards
- Assessment of evidence of prior achievements can provide employees with credit towards a qualification and therefore recognition for their existing competence
- More effective links with training and education providers can be made with external provision being matched to both company and individual needs.

General guidance

The issue of standards of performance has been the basis of considerable debate and development in the last decade. Many companies have undertaken work to develop their own standards. When considering whether to introduce national standards, a key point to keep in mind is that national standards of occupational competence provide a *benchmark across the sector*.

Using national standards within the company provides a basis for *consistency*, not just within your own organisation, but in other organisations across the sector. There is no reason why you should not 'enhance' national standards to incorporate your own company standards, but if you want to provide access to NVQs for your employees, you must ensure that the core of nationally agreed standards remains intact.

Once the system of NVQs has been operational for some time, it is expected that recruitment will be facilitated. Units of competence and NVQs will provide the currency by which employers will be able to identify what potential employees can do and in which areas they will need further development.

The issue of increased flexibility was outlined earlier. This is perhaps one of the key benefits for employers who can use competence-based standards as a foundation for cost-effective training needs analysis and total flexibility in delivery of training.

Strategic issues – should we introduce standards and NVQs?

- In what ways do we perceive that the introduction of competence-based standards would contribute to improvement of company performance?
- Are we introducing ISO 9000 and/or TQM? How would introducing competence-based standards fit in with these plans?
- How would these changes affect job roles and responsibilities?
- Would the introduction of NVQs conflict with any existing company qualification or incentive scheme?
- Do we already have company standards? If so, how will these integrate with national competence-based standards for relevant occupations?
- Which issues need to be discussed fully with trade unions?
- What initial costs (ie, registration fees, etc.) are payable to ILBs and/or awarding bodies?
- What other costs are involved?

Strategic issues – general guidance

Improvement of company performance
This issue must be decided on an in-company basis. A clear understanding of the new structure of standards and NVQs, and of their potential use within an organisation, is essential if informed decisions are to be made.

ISO 9000 and TQM
It is likely that competence-based standards will provide a complementary approach to the introduction of quality systems. New standards focus on outcomes of performance and on improving quality of individual contributions to company success.

Job roles
If explicit, accessible standards are to be introduced, one assumes they will be used to assess performance and not just to inform individuals of what their performance should be! This has implications for job roles. Who assesses? What extra responsibility/workload is this likely to create? (It should be minimal if a quality recording system is used. Standards should make explicit what line managers and supervisors are doing on a daily basis.)

Existing company qualifications/incentive schemes

If your company already operates an in-company certificate scheme, and particularly if this is linked to some form of incentive or bonus scheme, then you will need to consider how the introduction of NVQs fits in with these arrangements. Even if you are not currently operating such schemes, the issue of incentive/reward needs consideration – people's expectations may well link achievement of qualifications to promotion or other rewards.

Existing company standards

Your existing standards may be in a competence format or in some form of 'profile'. It is important to be clear about any differences between your existing standards and those which form the basis of NVQs (ie, national competence-based standards). There is no reason why you cannot enhance or 'contextualise' national standards to meet organisational needs, but if you wish to retain the link with the award of NVQs, the core of national standards must remain. In addition, simply adding on standards in another format may directly affect the assessment scheme. It is likely, therefore, that you will need some help in integrating company and national standards – or indeed 'contextualising' national standards for company use.

Trade unions

National standards have been developed by industry. Trade unions are usually fully represented on the development projects. However, some issues may arise and these will need to be dealt with by careful planning. For example, the question of assessors (first-line managers) being responsible for 'signing off' individuals as competent can be the cause of concern in some areas – particularly in those occupations where health and safety are priorities. Similarly, any changes in job roles may need full discussion with relevant trade unions.

Initial costs

For NVQs, the awarding bodies (sometimes ILBs as joint awarding bodies), charge an initial registration fee for 'centres' operating NVQs. (A centre can be a company or regions of a company for example.) Other implementation costs will include staff time for briefing/training and any development undertaken. The initial registration fee usually includes costs of materials (copies of standards, recording documents, etc).

Other costs
Other ongoing costs may include an annual registration fee (not all NVQs have this) and certification fees. Two forms of certification fee can be payable – one for a unit certificate and the other for a full NVQ. Unit certification costs vary, but average about £10 per certificate per person. Assistance with funding to help with the implementation of NVQs is available from TECs – see p. 139.

Development and implementation costs – general
The chart in Figure 4.1 is taken from *Competence and Assessment* (Training Agency 1988/90) and illustrates the key points to consider for development, start-up and implementation of standards.

Initial planning – how do we start?

■ Do we introduce the use of standards in association with NVQs? If not, how will we assess in-company?
■ What are the implications of first-line managers becoming assessors?
 – What training will they need?
 – What about legal responsibility for signing off an employee as competent (eg, health/safety)?
 – What support will they need?
■ What are the key occupational roles in our organisation?
■ In which occupational areas would individuals and the company both benefit most from the introduction of NVQs?
■ Who are the ILBs in the appropriate occupational areas?
■ Are national standards available for these occupational roles?
■ Are NVQs available in all occupational areas relevant to our needs?
■ How relevant are national standards to our work roles?
■ Do we want to contextualise the national standards to incorporate our company's objectives or company-specific standards?
■ Who awards the NVQs in these areas? Do we have any existing arrangements with those awarding bodies?
■ How would we motivate staff to operate to the specified standards?
■ Should we consider a phased introduction? Which occupational areas would offer the best test-bed site for a cost-effective implementation?
■ In which occupational area would we introduce standards first?
■ How will we ensure maintenance of standards?

[A] COSTS IN DEVELOPMENT

- **costs to the organisation co-ordinating development:**
  (normally an Industry Lead Body)

  * personnel – within the organisation at senior, intermediate, clerical, and secretarial grades, and at technical staff grades
  * staff travel – to participate in meetings, etc
  * internal copying, etc
  * meetings – travel and subsistence of participants catering (whether external or internal) accommodation charges
  * consultants fees – to assist in the proper application of the development strategy
  * printing – to present drafts etc for consultation
  * postage/telephone – for communicating with other participants in the development
  * computer development – any costs associated with developing programmes to record results of analysis
  * computer processing – processing data from development

- **costs to organisations providing 'technical' expertise to the development (normally industry, individual practitioners, ILEA's)**

  * Personnel – within the organisation at senior, intermediate, clerical and secretarial grades and at technical staff grades
  * internal copying, etc
  * postage/telephone – for communicating with other participants in the development

- **costs to awarding/accrediting bodies**

  * personnel – within the organisation at senior, intermediate, clerical and secretarial grades and at technical staff grades
  * internal copying, etc
  * postage/telephone – for communicating with other participants in the development

- **costs to industry**

  * personnel – within the organisation at senior, intermediate, clerical and secretarial grades and at technical staff grades
  * internal copying, etc
  * postage/telephone – for communicating with other participants in the development

[B] COSTS IN START-UP

* Same ranges and heads of costs to [A], and in addition to costs under A
* NCVQ – accreditation of award in principle (so, same range of cost heads as for others apply)
* industry, LIB – training of participants in implementing the system (NOT Training the individuals who will be assessed under the system)
* awarding bodies – participation in training of participants, associated administrative and clerical costs

[C] COSTS IN IMPLEMENTATION

* Same ranges and heads of costs in [A] and [B], and in addition to costs under A & B
* Industry people time dedicated to any stage or level with assessment
  - recording with review of candidate performance
  - coping with errors of competence attribution or mis-attribution

Figure 4.1 Assessing costs: (a) development of standards, (b) start-up costs, (c) implementation

DERBY COLLEGE : WILMORTON
LIBRARY

Initial planning – general guidance

Can we introduce standards without introducing NVQs?
Standards have many uses within an organisation, but are of key importance in improving company performance. This can only be achieved if the standards are used within a quality assessment scheme. Providing access to national vocational qualifications may well be a motivational factor for employees and also provides a quality assessment scheme. Companies should develop their own assessment recording systems (see Fletcher 1997c).

First-line managers as assessors
The extension of line managers' roles may have implications which need discussion with trade unions. (See 'Job roles' and 'Trade unions' in the previous section on strategic issues.) Assessors will certainly need training in the use of competence-based standards and assessment. Support systems will also need to be considered, both for the benefit of assessors and for the maintenance of standards.

Key occupational roles
You will need to complete an 'occupational mapping exercise'. Remember, standards and NVQs are to be available across all occupations of all sectors of all industries.

Priority areas
You will need to consider the benefits to both individuals and company based on current operational requirements and plans.

Availability of standards
ILBs will be able to provide this information. You can obtain a full list of ILBs in the *NCVQ Monitor*, available from NCVQ.

Availability of NVQs
The NCVQ publishes a bi-monthly bulletin of new NVQs and all information is stored on the NCVQ database.

Relevance of national standards
You will need to obtain copies of published standards in order to make this decision. Again, ILBs or the NCVQ database will provide this information. Alternatively awarding bodies publications lists will prove a useful source for purchasing copies.

Contextualising standards

If you feel that national standards are not entirely relevant, or that your company standards need to be added to this national benchmark, there is no reason why this cannot be done. However, if you wish to maintain access to NVQs the national standards must remain as the core of assessment. You may need help to do this.

Funding

Check with your local Training and Enterprise Council regarding possible financial support for implementation of NVQs (this changes each year).

Awarding bodies

As explained in Chapter 1, our traditional perceptions of an awarding body, such as City & Guilds or BTEC, need to change. Where once the syllabus and examination leading to an award (ie, a qualification) were their responsibility, they nowadays incorporate standards set by industry into a qualification framework set by the NCVQ. They have overall responsibility for the quality of assessment, but not for assessment methods.

In addition, some ILBs (see Chapter 2) are now also partners in the award structure and have taken on the newly defined awarding body role. NVQs may therefore be awarded by one of the familiar national bodies, or jointly with an ILB. See the *NVQ Monitor*, published by NCVQ, for a full listing of awarding bodies.

Motivating staff

You will need to identify the key benefits for each group of staff and consider how you will sell the idea of standards and NVQs. Communication networks need careful consideration.

Phased introduction

It is probably best to identify priority areas for introduction of standards and NVQs – perhaps admin and clerical staff, or managers, first, or a key technical area. A clear plan to cover the workforce is essential.

Maintenance of standards

Qualifications submitted to the NCVQ for approval will have an associated assessment model and quality control mechanism. The awarding bodies have overall responsibility for assessment and quality (as it is they who award the qualification). An awarding body moderator (external verifier) will visit the company on a regular basis (or a sample of companies) to check that the assessment system is operating as it should. You should also consider providing in-company support in the form of countersigning officers (who monitor the work of a number of assessors and countersign completed units of competence).

You might also consider regular meetings for assessors to enable them to exchange information and ideas in a peer group environment. This could be combined with, for instance, work on quality circles, or regular departmental meetings.

Operational issues – what needs to be done?

- Who will be responsible for checking the relevance of standards to our operations?
- Who will undertake contextualisation of national standards if we feel this to be necessary?
- Who takes responsibility for the planning of introduction of standards
  - across the company?
  - in occupational sectors?
  - in departments?
- Who will be the assessors?
- Who needs to be trained?
- Who trains staff to understand and use standards?
- What lead time should we allow for the introduction of standards?
- What lead time do we need to allow for
  - briefing of all staff?
  - training of assessors?
- How much of this time would be allocated to
  - development?
  - training?
  - piloting?
- Who will be responsible for the design of training programmes which incorporate national standards? Do they need training?

Operational issues – general guidance

Checking relevance of standards

You will need to ensure that whoever undertakes this task has a clear understanding of competence-based standards and their use and is also well versed in the occupational area. You might consider workshops of relevant staff led by someone (internal or external) who has relevant competence-based experience. Alternatively, some TECs will fund an 'NVQ audit' and action plan.

Completing contextualisation

As noted in previous sections, it is probable that you will require external help with this work, unless you have an expert in-house. It is important to ensure that the format of 'enhanced standards' does not detract from the quality of the associated assessment scheme.

Planning the introduction of standards

Responsibility for the planned introduction of standards must be given to someone who understands what must be done, has the expertise required and is allocated adequate time to control and monitor the process. A hierarchical structure might be adopted with each division or department having a responsible officer who reports to a senior manager.

Designing your assessment recording system

Keep it simple! Portfolios are not a requirement. Link NVQ assessment directly to your existing assessment and appraisal systems. For further help see Fletcher (1997c).

Deciding on assessors

This is a key decision. Assessors must have sufficient contact with candidates to be able to make a fair and confident judgement of competent performance. They must also, wherever possible, be willing to undertake the role – reluctant assessors will not undertake quality assessment.

Who needs to be trained?

Anyone who will be using the standards for assessment purposes will need to be trained in the principles and concepts of competence-based assessment, and the use of occupational standards. They will also need to understand the procedures associated with the assessment system. If trainers are to be involved in the redesign of training programmes, they will need training in competence-based design. A general briefing and information-providing session for the company as a whole would also be a good idea!

Who trains staff to understand and use standards?

As with all training, you have the choice. Some ILBs provide training, some external training providers have expertise in this area. Be clear about the purpose of training: is it briefing on competence-based standards generally, or occupationally specific training you need?

Lead time

This will depend on how many occupational areas are involved in your implementation plan and whether you are planning a phased introduction. Most companies find that the lead time to actual operation of NVQs is longer than their original estimates. Again, this varies if you are contextualising standards.

Design of training programmes

If you plan to redesign your in-company training programmes, your own trainers will need training in competence-based design. If you use external providers, make sure they can design training to the competence-based standards you are using.

Further development – how will we use the standards throughout the company?

- Do we have a performance appraisal system? Would we want to redesign this to incorporate national standards?
- Do we have a training policy?
- Do we have a strategic training plan?
- Is our current training plan based on a standards approach?
- Is our current recruitment/manpower planning strategy based on a standards approach?

Further development – general guidance

Performance appraisal

As you are considering the introduction of in-company assessment leading to NVQs, it makes sense to consider how this links with any existing, or planned, performance appraisal system. This will require a review of the current system and an examination of how competence-based standards of performance can be incorporated into current procedures.

You might consider whether formative assessment (ie, over time, on a continuous basis) will contribute to the summative assessment (annual performance appraisal and report).

Training policy and strategic plan

If you have a current training policy and strategic plan, this will need review based on redesigned training programmes and procedures which will accompany the introduction of NVQs. With a competence-based system, you will have more flexibility in training delivery: training needs can be identified on an ongoing basis, as part of normal assessment procedures. How will you make best use of this flexibility in your annual training plans?

Recruitment and manpower planning

You may want to consider how you can use the standards to redraft recruitment specifications and to facilitate forecasting of future manpower needs. The units of competence will give you a clear idea of the functions carried out in your organisation; this information can also assist with plans for multiskilling or for the introduction of new plant and technology.

4.2 NVQs AND TRAINING PROGRAMMES

At the risk of labouring a point, it is probably still worth reminding you that NVQs are concerned with *assessment of workplace performance* and not with training programmes.

Many companies, even those which are beginning to introduce NVQs, still ask how they can get their training programmes accredited by the NCVQ. The short answer is *you can't!*

However, if your in-company training programmes are revised so that they are based on nationally agreed standards of competence, they can, when combined with competence-based assessment, provide *evidence* of competence. Your programme can then be approved by a relevant accrediting institution (FE college, university) as providing *relevant knowledge and understanding* for NVQ units. Candidates will still need to *demonstrate the application* of this knowledge and understanding to achieve NVQ certification.

No doubt this sounds very confusing. This dilemma is indicative of the difficulty in switching one's thinking to accommodate the new nature of qualifications. You need to keep in mind that NVQs are not training programmes – units of competence are not units (or modules) of training, but units of *assessment*. If your training programmes include assessment of competence (ie, performance), then this assessment is providing evidence of competence. You will recall that competence-based assessment requires *sufficient* evidence of competence performance – sufficient for a confident judgement to be made. This evidence will come from many sources, including performance assessed in the course of training programmes.

Individuals do not achieve NVQs by simply completing training or learning programmes, they achieve them by demonstrating competence in a workplace environment.

INFORMATION SECTION

Investors in People

The Investors in People initiative (IiP) was launched in 1990 and requires participating companies to make a 'public commitment from the top to develop all employees to achieve its business objectives'.

Delivered via Training and Enterprise Councils (TECs), the IiP initiative sets out a methodology for achieving the award which includes the establishment of a written business plan and consideration of how employees will contribute to meeting specific goals and targets. Managers and employees must regularly agree training needs and resources must be allocated.

To date, more than 400 companies have been recognised as Investors in People, while another 4000 are committed to achieving the standard.

The initiative was launched with a briefing pack, which contained three key documents. Briefing document 1 was for board members, senior managers and business development and marketing staff in Training and Enterprise Councils (Local Enterprise Councils in Scotland). This first document provided the 'context' for the initiative, summarising the business issues which strategically drove the focus for its introduction.

The second briefing document described the framework of Investors in People and detailed the principles and action points embodied within it.

The third document was entitled 'The Proof' and provided examples of companies who were already developing their people as an investment (rather than a cost, as is traditionally the case).

The objectives of Investors in People are as follows:

To encourage companies to adopt a planned, business-led approach to investing in people, by demonstrating the business rationale for, and benefits of, this approach.

To help companies commit to investing in the people in their company, by adopting the principles and actions embodied in the national standard. Companies seeking to achieve the Investor in People status will be required to make a public commitment to this goal.

To reward companies which have met the national standard and are able to demonstrate this approach working successfully in their business. TECs and LECs are able to award a kitemark, to proclaim that a company has achieved the status of an Investor in People.

IiP briefing document 2, Employment Department 1990

Understandably, the use of the term 'national standard' presented some confusion when the initiative was first introduced. Most people were still getting used to national standards being the basis of NVQs – and here was another national standard to take on board.

Since its initial introduction, IiP has also been linked directly with NVQs and the Investors initiative is used as a means for accelerating the implementation of NVQs (and vice versa).

The initiative is based on four fundamental principles, which must be followed – it is these four principles which form the national standard for IiP:

- An Investor in People makes a public commitment from the top to develop all employees to achieve its business objectives.
- An Investor in People regularly reviews the training and development needs of all employees.
- An Investor in People takes action to train and develop individuals on recruitment and throughout their employment.
- An Investor in People evaluates the investment in training and development to assess achievement and improve future effectiveness.

Achieving the award

In order to achieve the Investors in People award, an organisation must undergo an assessment. Standards (or organisational competences) are made explicit and evidence must be provided to meet these standards which were revised in 1996. Advisers and assessors will be appointed by your local TEC/LEC.

Advisers and assessors for IiP are trained (for example by Henley Management College) and must themselves achieve approved status. Once approved, IiP advisers and assessors register with a TEC/LEC and can then be allocated to companies to undertake the advisory and assessment roles.

Employers are provided with a 'diagnostic pack' and the adviser will go through the required standards and help to compile relevant evidence. An approved IiP assessor will then review this evidence. IiP assessors are themselves judged against standards which are based on the national (NVQ) assessor standards.

An IiP assessor uses a workbook which contains all the relevant standards to be met by the organisation aiming to achieve the award.

Further details of the Investors in People award and how to achieve it can be obtained from your local Training and Enterprise Council, or Local Enterprise Council in Scotland.

5

Planning for Assessment and Certification

INTRODUCTION

In order to plan your NVQ system, you must consider all aspects of assessment of performance. You must also discard any previous assumptions about 'assessment'. Competence-based assessment requires a change in traditional thinking. By exploring issues with an open mind, you will be able to make full use of the potential of the NVQ system – and reap all the added-value benefits of an integrated performance management system.

Key criteria to keep in mind in respect of your NVQ system are:

- Business-led
- Fit for purpose(s)
- User-friendly
- Flexible.

This chapter outlines key differences between competence-based assessment and traditional assessment, opening your range of planning to consider new options.

You will also find guidance on how competence-based assessment works in principle, giving you a basis to explore ideas.

After reading this chapter, I suggest you revisit Chapter 4 and begin your planning process in earnest.

Chapter 11 provides you with detail on implementation of your assessment system.

5.1 WHAT IS ASSESSMENT?

This may seem like a very obvious question, but try writing a brief answer for yourself. When you have completed this, try the following questions:

- What do you know/do about assessment of:
    - your company's performance?
    - your department's performance?
    - your section's performance?
    - your unit's performance?
    - individual performance?
    - your own performance?
- How do you assess:
    - training needs?
    - effectiveness of training in your organisation?
- What measures do you use/your company use to assess all of the above?

(See also Fletcher 1997a)

Let's try a related area – *certification*. When recruiting staff, do you look for staff with particular qualifications (ie, certificates, diplomas, etc)? Do you know how individuals are assessed in order to achieve those qualifications? You might also consider what the qualification tells you about the individual.

When you have completed this exercise for yourself, you might like to try the questions on other people within your organisation and compare the answers.

Personal perceptions

The term 'assessment' can be interpreted in many ways. If we talk about 'assessment of the company's performance', we could be considering measures such as profitability, market share, productivity. Assessment of department or unit performance may lead us to talk about 'qualitative and quantitative measures' and discussions about 'objectives' and 'targets'.

Assessment of individual performance, in a company context, usually refers to systems for 'performance appraisal' – which, sadly, are themselves often an annual ritual rather than an effective measure – or the term might be reminiscent of periods spent at an 'assessment centre' where various tasks, games and discussions led to a form of management profiling.

Quite often, 'assessment of individual performance' is also seen as the domain of occupational psychologists with arms full of psychometric tests and personal files.

A traditional view

Our personal perceptions of assessment are probably shaped by our own experiences of being assessed or assessing. In general, most people's experience of assessment is by formal testing of some kind, whether it be a written examination, verbal report or a form of skills test.

We may all have carried out some form of assessment ourselves, perhaps without even realising it – an interview situation is a prime example of this. Interviewers make an assessment (or judgement) about interviewees based on documentation and discussion, perhaps with a skills test thrown in.

Traditional forms of assessment follow a pattern of formalised assessment – and usually have formalised measures to use in making judgements. For example, let's consider the traditional form of assessment for a vocational qualification:

student registers for and undertakes
specific course of study/training

student completes course assignments
which are assessed by tutors
(written or skills tests)

student takes final examination
or presents dissertation/thesis.

Table 5.1 outlines the measures that are used.

Most traditional assessment methods use a percentage pass mark. Most are also *norm referenced*, ie, individual results are compared with the results of others based on a 'normal' or expected pass rate. Figure 5.1 illustrates what this actually means in practice.

While a well-designed learning programme aims to provide all the input (often combined with practical experience) needed to cover a specific vocational area, this traditional form of assessment results in a final grading which represents assessment on perhaps only half of the actual skills, knowledge and understanding that are required.

Many education and training providers have moved forward from this very traditional position and have improved collaboration with employers in order to make learning and assessment more relevant to the actual work role. However, while percentage pass marks remain there will always be questions like 'In which areas was this individual not assessed?' 'Which areas did this individual choose to avoid in the examination?' 'Were any of these areas critical to competent performance?'

Table 5.1 Traditional measures of achievement in vocational qualifications

Assessment method	Measure
Course assignments	50% pass
Final examination/thesis	50% pass

Competence-based assessment

New forms of assessment (an integral part of NVQs), differ from the traditional approaches in six key areas:

1. a foundation of outcome-based standards
2. individualised assessment
3. competent/not yet competent judgements only (not percentage pass marks)
4. assessment in the workplace
5. no specified time for completion of assessment
6. no specified course of learning/study.

In competence-based assessment, it is *individual performance* which is judged – and judged against explicit standards which reflect not what that individual should know, but the *expected outcomes* of that individual's *competent performance*. How individuals perform in comparison to others is irrelevant.

Only two judgements can be made: either the person has consistently demonstrated workplace performance which meets the specified

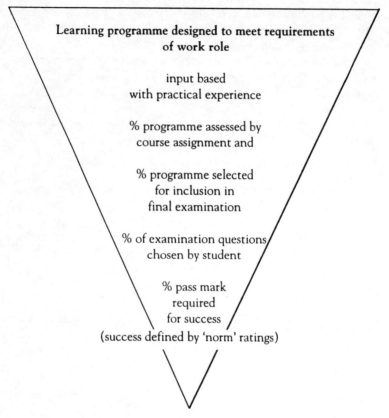

Figure 5.1 Traditional assessment procedures

standards or they are not yet able to do so – 'competent', or 'not yet competent'.

Individuals are assessed in the workplace wherever possible. If assessment is undertaken in connection with the company's implementation of NVQs, individuals will achieve units of competence (and eventually a whole NVQ) at their own pace.

Competence-based standards are available to assessors and assessees. Individuals know exactly what they are aiming to achieve and assessors can provide specific feedback. Ongoing assessment uses normal workplace performance as its basis, and this continuous assessment process helps in the identification of training needs.

Individuals do not attend a specified course of study (unless the company wishes to provide this). Learning can take place on the job, through formal in-company or external courses, through open learning or, indeed, any method which meets both company and individual needs. Training can be targeted to individual needs.

What is being assessed?

Consistency is of prime importance. A one-off demonstration of skill (as in a skills test) is not sufficient for making a judgement about competent performance. As an employer or manager, you need people who can perform in their work role to a *consistently* high standard.

Standards defined in a competence format, as described in Chapter 3, are explicit descriptions of the expected outcomes of workplace activity. When using these standards as a framework for the design of an assessment system, that framework establishes that it is the outcomes of individual performance that will be judged by assessors.

Who assesses?

The primary method of assessment in a competence-based system is *observation of workplace performance*. If assessment uses explicit standards of occupational performance as its foundation, then the logical way to assess whether someone is meeting those standards is to watch them working in that occupation.

The next logical conclusion is, of course, that the best people to assess are workplace supervisors or first-line managers – people who have first-hand and regular contact with the individuals who are being assessed.

For those companies which have identified the benefits of introducing total quality management (TQM) and ISO 9000,* an assessment system which demands involvement of line managers throughout the organisational structure is perfectly in accord with organisational aims and objectives. One can also argue that this form of assessment simply makes explicit what supervisors and first-line managers should be doing anyway.

However, the implications of introducing competence-based assessment (and NVQs) need careful consideration and planning.

---

* Companies which have been accredited with ISO 9000 have undergone an audit of their quality policy, systems and control. ISO 9000 includes quality systems, standards and guidelines that complement relevant product or service technical specifications.

5.2 HOW IS COMPETENCE-BASED ASSESSMENT CONDUCTED?

We have briefly considered the 'what' and 'who' of both new and traditional competence-based assessment. For most companies which are interested in using new forms of standards and/or qualifications, a prime question is the 'how'.

All assessment is about collecting and judging *evidence*. For the tutor/assessor on a traditional college-based vocational programme, the actual forms of evidence collected are completed course work and assignments and final examination results.

For the workplace assessor, operating within a competence-based assessment system, the actual products of performance provide *evidence* to be matched against specified standards. A workplace assessor will seek evidence of performance which matches the element, performance criteria and range statement for each unit of competence. Where evidence is not available from normal working practice, or would be difficult to generate, the assessor may need to set up supplementary assessments.

For example, a competent worker may be one who is able to deal with a number of contingencies – machine breakdown, sudden changes in workload or priorities, or even a fire. It would obviously not be practicable for an assessor to cause a deliberate breakdown of machinery (or indeed set fire to the building), simply to assess an individual's ability to cope. In this context, therefore, an assessor needs to be skilled in providing opportunities for supplementary assessment. This may involve a skills test, questioning of the individual, or allocating a new task or job.

A workplace assessor requires training in the use of competence-based standards, and in the application of various assessment methods. It is the workplace assessor who 'signs off' an individual as competent, and he/she needs to be confident in this role. National standards and unit awards are available for assessors and 'accredited' assessors are required to operate the NVQ system (see NCVQ 1997).

What about quality control?

Any system of standards will only be as good as the quality control mechanism that ensures they are maintained. Within competence-based assessment systems, and particularly within those that lead to award of NVQs, quality control is a prerequisite to operational approval. For NVQs, various systems are in place, but all follow a basic pattern in which the workplace assessors are supported and monitored by *internal and external verifiers*.

In terms of external quality control the awarding bodies have overall responsibility for assessment within NVQs; they award units and full qualifications. External verifiers support and monitor workplace assessors.

Internal quality control is the concern of internal verifiers – in company 'countersigning officers' – and workplace assessors like supervisors and first-line managers. In 1993, NCVQ and the awarding bodies published a Common Accord (revised 1997) which aimed to provide consistency in quality assurance across all NVQs.

5.3 NEW FORMS OF CERTIFICATION

What do certificates tell us?

We have already reviewed the traditional pattern of formalised assessment leading to the award of a certificate, diploma, or other form of vocational qualification. At the beginning of this chapter, you were asked to consider a number of questions, one of them being 'What does a qualification tell you about an individual?'

Traditional qualifications usually tell us that the qualification holder has passed the formal assessment process. They may also indicate that the individual has achieved a pass, credit or distinction. This, of course, relates to the percentage pass mark achieved, which, as we noted earlier, is norm-referenced.

NVQ certificates

Let's consider another question: 'What would a new NVQ tell you about an individual?'

A qualification with the NCVQ logo will tell us that the qualification holder has passed the assessment process. It will not include a pass, credit or distinction grading because for NVQs these grades do not exist. It will also tell us that the assessment process involved assessment of actual performance in the workplace as the primary form of assessment. The certificate will also show the *units of competence* which the certificate holder has achieved.

Now consider an interview scenario. A candidate for an interview presents you with copies of 'credits towards an NVQ'. What does this tell you about the candidate?

Under the new national 'credit accumulation scheme', individuals will accumulate credits towards a full NVQ, each credit being a unit of competence. Awarding bodies will provide certificates on a unit level which can be 'exchanged' for a full NVQ once the relevant total of units has been achieved.

5.4 BENEFITS OF A CREDIT ACCUMULATION SYSTEM

- Easier access to qualifications
- Units can be built up over time
- Trainees are motivated by immediate recognition of their achievements
- Units from different awarding bodies can be brought together in one place
- Integration of different parts of a learning programme and different modes of learning
- Tutors and trainers will be able to operate within a common system
- More flexible learning programmes can be designed
- A clear statement of the holder's competence is provided in language familiar to employers
- It can record credits from one learning programme to another, throughout life
- Acceleration of progress towards a competence-based national system of qualifications.

5.5 ACCREDITATION OF PRIOR LEARNING (APL)

The accreditation of prior learning (APL) permits the award of credit towards a qualification on the basis of evidence drawn from an individual's past achievements (City & Guilds 1990)

The accreditation of prior learning (APL) is an *integral* part of assessment for NVQs. It is a process in which evidence of an individual's past achievements within a relevant occupational role can be judged against the standards specified within the appropriate vocational qualification.

Evidence from past achievements must satisfy the requirements of the specified qualification, but can take many forms. Direct evidence of achievement includes 'products' of performance – ie, actual outcomes of the individual's work activity. Indirect evidence includes information 'about the individual', such as performance reports, letters from satisfied customers and the like.

The process for assessment of evidence of past achievement differs from any other competence-based assessment only in the preparatory stages. Individual candidates must take responsibility for collecting together evidence which is valid and authentic and matches the specified standards. Initial guidance from a trained adviser will be needed at this stage.

APL and 'skills audit'

The importance of APL at national level relates to the overall objective of widening access to assessment for vocational qualifications, especially among adults who have a wealth of skill and experience and do not necessarily wish to undertake lengthy periods of study.

The credit accumulation system on which NVQs are based makes the APL approach particularly attractive to a wide audience. If 'credit' for existing competence is available, then education, training and development need be targeted only to remedy gaps in occupational competence.

At company level, this last point is probably of most interest. Better targeted training means less 'downtime', and a higher return on investment in training.

A company's workforce can be awarded credit towards nationally recognised qualifications, without having to attend any form of training or learning programme, purely on the basis of evidence of what they can actually do now. This itself is often a motivational aspect for the introduction of both standards and NVQs, providing benefits for both employer and employees.

A note on 'portfolios'

It is *not* a requirement of the NVQ system that candidates collect evidence in a 'portfolio'. This is a time-consuming and costly exercise. Candidates must *demonstrate* competent performance – 'performance evidence' demonstrates 'can-do' – which is best assessed by observation, by review of products of performance and by questioning (see Fletcher 1997c and NCVQ 1997).

—— 6 ——

Identifying the Right NVQs

This chapter provides guidance on collecting the right information, from the right people, at the right time.

So, where do you start?

Logically, if you are going to implement standards, or NVQs based on standards, you must first obtain those standards. To obtain standards, you must first decide in which occupational areas you need them. Your local Training and Enterprise Council may help with this initial research through a funded 'NVQ Audit'.

IDENTIFYING OCCUPATIONAL AREAS

Perhaps your company has already conducted an occupational mapping exercise. You may even have clear management direction about which occupations are to be used as a pilot, or as the initial implementation areas. However, let's consider implementation from the beginning and look at what needs to be done to identify these initial or pilot areas.

What is the key occupation in your organisation?

This should relate to your organisation's *key purpose* or *mission statement*.

The term 'occupation' refers to a key area of work – for example, administrative and clerical, process engineering, management, training and development: all are occupations.

It is important to recognise that occupations, as defined within the Standards Development Programme, may cross traditional boundaries of vocational training and practice. Units of competence defined for a specified occupation may be used in a number of different industries.

The following list catalogues occupational areas as defined by the

National Council for Vocational Qualifications. This can be used as a checklist for your organisation.

Occupational areas

Accountancy
Agriculture
Air transport
Amenity horticulture
Animal care
Architecture
Arts/performing arts
Armed forces
Baking
Banking
Basket making
Biscuit, cake, chocolate
Boat building
Blacksmiths
Books
Brushes
Building maintenance/estate
   management
Building societies
Bus and coach
Business administration
Care
Carpets
Electronic office
Energy management
Engineering
Engineering construction
Engineering/profess
Envelope makers
Estate agents
Extractive industries
Fibre board/packing
Film making, TV, video
Fire service
Flexible packaging
Floristry
Food manufacture

Caravanning and leisure parks
Cement
Ceramics
Chemicals
Chimney sweeps
Civil service
Claypipes/refractories
Cleaning
Clothing
Concrete
Conservation
Construction
Cosmetics
Cotton/allied products
Crafts/enterprise
Dairy
Design
Drinks
Dry cleaners/launderers
Education
Electrical contracting
Electrical services
Electricity
Knitting and lace
Languages
Law
Leather processing
Light leathergoods
Leather – saddle/bridle
Local government
Locksmiths
Management/supervisory
Man-made fibres
Merchant navy
Meat
Millers
Mining (including coke)

Footwear manufacture
Footwear repair
Forensic science
Forestry
Fresh produce
Furniture
Gamekeeping/fish husbandry
Garden/agric. machinery
Gas
Glass
Guidance/counselling
Hairdressing
Hand/machine knitting
Health and beauty
Health and safety
Horses
Hotel and catering
Housing
Information technology
IT – constructive users
IT – practitioners
Inland waterways
Insurance
International trade
Jewellery
Retail travel
Road transport
Rubber
Sales
Screen printers
Sea fishing
Security
Shipbuilding
Signmaking
Soap and detergent
Small businesses
Small tool/plant hire
Sound
Sport and recreation
Steel

Museums, galleries/heritage
Narrow fabrics
Newspapers
Nuclear
Office skills
Offshore oil
Packaging
Paint
Paper and board
Pensions management
Periodicals
Personnel management
Petrol refining
Pharmaceuticals
Photography
Plastics
Police
Ports and harbours
Post Office
Printing
Printing ink
Prisons
Purchasing and supply
Railways
Retail
Sugar
Telecommunications
Textile manufacture
Thatching
Theatre technicians
Timber
Tobacco
Tourism and leisure
Training and development
Wall covering
Wastes management
Water
Wholesale
Wire and wire rope
Wool

The above list includes occupational areas where Industry Lead Bodies (see Chapter 1) have been established.

What are the key occupational roles within your organisation?

This question may present a little more difficulty, as it requires a shift of thinking. The traditional way of thinking about standards is to relate them to *jobs* – but the same job can have many different titles. In addition, there are many jobs within an *occupation*.

The usual source of information regarding work roles within a organisation is the personnel department. You will need to review the information available – but be careful about using job descriptions or job specifications since these outline individual job titles, not occupational roles.

Examples of occupational roles may include supervisor, technician, operative or trainer.

Remember, when considering key occupational roles, to think in broader terms than the key occupation of your organisation. The key occupation may be manufacturing, or processing, or one of the service industries, but key occupational roles will include the *range* and levels of activity undertaken within the organisation.

What supporting occupations occur within your organisation?

To make sure that you include all organisational activities, don't forget to list the managerial, administrative or unskilled roles that support your organisation's main function. If you work in a very large company, many different roles contribute to effective operations.

Are you introducing standards across the board or in key occupations only?

Having established a clear 'occupational map', you now need to be clear about which occupational areas to address first. In general, organisations tend to introduce competence-based standards and NVQs in the key occupational areas (and key occupational roles) for the initial, pilot phase. In this way, the contribution to improved performance can be judged directly in relation to key areas of performance. However, supporting occupations can also play a key part in successful performance, and your company's decision will be based on consideration of implications and benefits in relation to operational objectives.

IDENTIFYING STANDARDS

Once you know the occupational areas in which you will be introducing standards and NVQs, the next problem is *finding* the standards.

Current work on development of national standards is gradually ensuring that these will be available in all occupational areas, but some sectors are way ahead of others. You need to find the answers to two key questions: Are national standards available for the identified key occupational areas? And how do these national standards relate to our needs?

Should the answer to the first of these be no, you then have to consider the following options: Do we wait until relevant national standards become available? Do we start work on our own competence-based standards? Are there draft national standards available which we can use as a foundation for our own developments? If we develop our own standards, how can we ensure that we can still link in with new NVQs when they become available?

Taking each of these questions in turn we'll consider

- how to get information
- what to do with the information when you have it
- implications of action.

Are national standards available for the identified key occupational areas?

In order to answer this question, you need to check with the providers of national standards – the ILB or with the providers of qualifications which incorporate these standards – the awarding bodies. This can be done in one of three ways:

- contact the ILB direct
- access the NCVQ database
- contact the awarding body.

You should not contact the NCVQ direct for information on standards.

A full list of current ILBs is available in the *NVQ Monitor*, published regularly by the NCVQ.

The NCVQ database is available on disc for access through a desk-top computer. It contains detailed information on all NVQs including the component units, elements and performance criteria and range statements (see Chapter 3 for explanations of these terms).

If standards are still under development, the awarding bodies will be involved in this work. Each has a publicity/information section and a catalogue of its qualifications. First identify the relevant awarding body from their catalogue of occupational qualifications and then contact their information office for details.

Your choice of approach will depend upon whether your company is planning to introduce NVQs as its key objective, or if your key interest is in *standards*. The NCVQ database lists only those NVQs which have been officially accredited (ie, after a contract between the relevant parties and the NCVQ has been signed). If you want to know the current state of play regarding development of standards (which will form the basis of new NVQs), then your best contact would be the ILB.

Let's assume that you have identified national standards (and NVQs) through the NCVQ database and/or through the ILB. As all national standards are published by ILBs, you can obtain a hard copy of the relevant standards and assessment guidance and check their applicability within your own organisation. This brings us to the next question.

How do these national standards relate to our needs?

National standards of occupational competence are developed to provide a benchmark of competent performance within a specified sector. Some developments, such as management competences or those for the training and development fields, are more 'generic' in nature; that is, they are used within a wide range of industry and commercial sectors. However, they will have been developed and tested through consultation with key role holders within defined areas of competence.

A key point about this sector-specific development relates both to mobility and exchangeability of the workforce. By introducing a common standard across each sector (and ensuring that the quality of assessment to those standards is maintained), it should be possible to create an employment environment in which recruitment, selection, manpower planning, etc. can be conducted on a common basis. Instead of having different standards between regions, or between companies, employers will be able to use the new certification (qualification) scheme as a hallmark of individuals' achievements.

Some companies have found, however, that the benchmark of competence, while serving the 'exchangeability' function quite adequately, is not sufficient for their own corporate purposes. Reasons for this perceived inadequacy include:

- the desire to incorporate the company's mission statement and objectives into operational standards
- the organisation's specific culture
- the organisation's commitment to excellence
- previously specified company standards.

This is not to say that new competence-based standards are not applicable – simply that they may need 'enhancing' or 'contextualising' in order to meet the organisational requirements.

There is no reason why this cannot be done, as long as the enhanced standards use the national standards as a core and retain the same format. Similarly, the associated assessment system must retain its quality and meet national criteria – as well as your company's operational needs. It is quite likely, therefore, that you will need help in achieving this contextualisation. This is a cost implication that must be considered.

You may, of course, decide that the published national standards completely meet your needs, and that you can introduce the units of competence (see Chapter 3) as they stand. If this is the case, you are in the lucky position of being able to move forward to the next chapter!

It is probably fair to say, however, that having identified the published standards for relevant occupational areas and roles, some difficulties will be encountered. Some units may be completely relevant while others are not.

There is no reason why you should introduce *all* the units from a defined NVQ. There is no point in trying to assess people in areas of work for which they have no responsibility, interest or even skill. The point of a credit-accumulation system is that units of competence are accessible individually. The NVQ framework will combine a number of units into a qualification. Your company may wish to introduce a mixture of units from a range of occupational roles – and even to negotiate with an awarding body to establish a new NVQ in a specialised area. Following the Beaumont Report (1996) there is more flexibility at national level to incorporate this 'pick and mix' approach.

What if national standards and/or NVQs are not yet available? Do we wait until relevant national standards become available?

The latter question can only be answered in relation to your company's reasons for introducing competence-based standards. What is the senior management directive on this issue? How urgent is the introduction of standards? For what reasons?

Much will depend on the current state of play in standards development. You can contact the ILB for an up-to-date picture and proposed timescales for production of national standards. This will at least provide you with the basis on which to make an informed decision.

Do we start work on our own competence-based standards?

You can do so, if the company is willing to invest time and money. You may already have company standards which you feel are competence-based. However, you should make sure you are familiar with the basic concepts and methodology involved in developing national competence-based standards (see Part I), before you make assumptions that your standards are in line with current developments.

The costs of development need careful consideration. Chapter 4 illustrated some of the cost headings involved in the development of national standards.

Are there draft national standards available which we can use as a foundation for our own developments?

This is quite likely to be the case. The ILB will be able to provide you with information. You should note, however, that most ILBs are reluctant to release draft versions of standards. This is because of the obvious assumption that providers and employers would use them for development of assessment and training programmes, only to find that the final, published version is drastically different!

You should therefore ensure that any draft material you intend to use has been field tested on at least one occasion.

Should you decide to take the route of developing your own company standards, it is likely that you will need consultancy support. Make sure you use a consultant who is fully *au fait* with national developments, including the technicalities of methodology. Taking a diverse (if cheaper) route can be less cost-effective in the long run.

If we develop our own standards, how can we ensure that we can still link in with new NVQs when they become available?

There is no reason why in-company standards (and assessment systems) should not meet national criteria, provided that careful liaison with national developments is maintained during the development process.

Awarding bodies need to be involved in the development stage; most will work with companies to establish a tailor-made qualification (this is essential in highly specialised areas anyway).

As you may have gathered by now, identifying occupational areas and standards is a key activity in the introduction of competence-based systems for measuring, monitoring and rewarding performance in the workplace. If standards are the foundation for improvement of performance then the foundation must be solid before any further action can be taken.

Get the standards right before taking any further action!

■ CASE STUDY ■

Automobile Association

Martin Churcher, Training Manager

BRIEF OVERVIEW OF THE ORGANISATION

The Automobile Association was founded in 1905 to protect the interests of its members. Ninety years later, it remains a non-profit-making and unincorporated members' club offering a wide range of products and services. The AA has nearly nine million members, more than five million customers, more than 12,000 staff and 40 different business activities.

The organisation is structured into four core businesses: AA Membership Services; AA Insurance, Retail and Financial Services; AA Commercial Services; and the Corporate Group.

Based in Basingstoke but operating nationally, the main aim of the AA Membership Business is to promote and provide service and assistance to its members.

REASONS FOR PLANNING TO INTRODUCE NVQs

The integration of NVQs and Investors in People into the business processes is a key element of the overall HR strategy. The Membership

Business sees NVQs as integral to the plans to use competence-based standards as part of an overall performance assessment process.

Perceived business benefits are:

- The standards-based structure of NVQs provide a consistent and nationally recognised set of performance measures.
- Better identification of training needs, thereby improving the cost-effectiveness of the training provision.
- Improvements in current job performance and preparation for future demands.
- Using line managers as assessors will enhance their role as coach to their teams.
- Improved motivation and increased flexibility of employees.

Perceived benefits for employees are:

- The standards-based structure of NVQs provides clear guidelines on the standards of performance expected within the role.
- The certification award would not only be viewed as a sense of achievement but its national status would give individuals a qualification, recognised and valued in the market place.
- NVQs can be incorporated into planned development for both staff and managers.

CONSIDERATIONS

There was growing interest from various areas of the business in adopting the NVQ approach, but rather than progress the possible introduction on an individual or ad hoc basis, the Business Board agreed to an audit to provide an overall strategic view of the relevance or otherwise of implementing an NVQ system. It was intended that the audit should also identify possible links with the Investors in People process which the business was also interested in exploring.

NVQs PLANNED/INTRODUCED

Which NVQs at which levels for which staff?

The audit conducted by Fletcher Consultancy and partly funded by the Hampshire TEC recommended, as a first step to introducing NVQs, that an in-house pilot scheme should run, initially for six months, and involve representatives from different areas of the business. The Customer Service Level 3 NVQ was recommended for the pilot.

This would enable the business to design and test an in-house assessment system and train and develop in-house assessors to gain assessor accreditation involving a number of areas in the business.

Who decided which NVQs individuals should take?

The initial NVQ audit had identified that the Customer Service NVQ Level 3 would be relevant to a number of areas and job roles. Using Customer Service Units would enable the business to pilot an NVQ in different business contexts.

This approach was fully supported by the Business Board.

PLANNING STAGE

A project manager from the business HR function was selected to work alongside the external consultant (Shirley Fletcher) and a plan produced to invite and select volunteers from across the business to take part as candidates, assessors and internal verifiers. There was some existing NVQ expertise in the business and these staff formed part of the internal verifier team.

Communication processes were set up to brief participants and managers, and an initial development session was organised for assessors and internal verifiers to discuss the objectives of the pilot, roles and processes, and introduce the documentation to be used during the pilot.

PILOTING

Assessors were allocated a number of candidates and the first task was for assessors and candidates to meet to discuss the process and the Customer Service standards and to prepare an assessment plan. Similarly, the internal verifier and assessors met to discuss assessment plans for the assessor candidates.

Candidates used a diary to record evidence from their daily work activities linked to the appropriate NVQ Unit and Element.

Progress of the pilot was controlled through a project group consisting of the project manager, external consultant and internal verifiers. This group met monthly to review progress, issue project updates and progress reports to participants and business managers, as well as supporting candidates and assessors.

PROGRESS/ISSUES

The launch of the pilot coincided with an unexpected heavy workload and this delayed the start in some areas, but once people got going good progress was made.

With practice, the majority of people found the documentation easy to use and suggestions for improvements were noted and incorporated into later versions. Many felt that the standards themselves would benefit from being presented in plain English, an issue also highlighted in the Beaumont Report.

The time needed to prepare plans and conduct candidates' assessments, again improved with practice, although the overall involvement time, for assessors particularly, was greater than expected. This was mainly because of time needed to get to the candidates' place of work and become familiar with the candidates' work activities.

The previous NVQ experience of two of the internal verifiers was mainly with a portfolio paper-led approach, a process we wanted to avoid.

DOCUMENTATION

The documentation was a key aspect of the pilot. It needed to be simple to use and suitable for a wide range of business contexts. In conjunction with Shirley Fletcher, specific in-house documents were developed which also reflected the latest guidelines. The documents consisted of:

■ an Evidence Diary – to enable candidates to record work activities and evidence;
■ a Workplace Assessment Report (WAR) – used both by assessors and internal verifiers to record progress of their respective candidates.

Comments on the documentation and suggestions for improvements to the assessment recording progress were noted as the pilot progressed and included in the feedback to internal verifiers, assessors and candidates. As a result a flexible recording process evolved.

Initially, some assessors asked for all the performance criteria to be listed as part of the assessment document, but because in some cases this led to the gathering of individual evidence for each performance criteria rather than 'packages of evidence', we excluded pre-printing these as part of the final document design.

QUALITY ASSURANCE

During the pilot, the internal verifiers monitored assessors and provided monthly reports to the Steering Group. In addition, a process was put in place by which a 100 per cent sample of assessor-candidate documentation and 20 per cent of all NVQ candidate documentation was reviewed.

External quality assurance was provided by Shirley Fletcher which enabled any issues arising to be addressed and fed back through the regular communication process. In addition, further development was provided to assessors as the pilot progressed.

Various questionnaires were used to provide mid-project and end-of-project feedback as part of the overall project evaluation process.

LESSONS LEARNED

- Communication and commitment are key to the successful use of NVQs. The use of a newsletter proved valuable as did using questionnaires to encourage feedback.
- The recording system needs to be flexible, easy to use and relevant to the context in which it is being applied. This calls for planning time to be allocated to ensure NVQs integrate with any existing performance recording systems and processes.
- Before introducing an NVQ the structure and content should be reviewed to ensure it is relevant and applicable to the occupational group concerned, and any necessary modifications made.
- Because of their regular contact with individuals, line managers are in the best position to undertake the assessor role.
- Assessors are key players in the NVQ process and adequate arrangements for their development and support must be in place.
- A prescriptive approach was shown to be inappropriate and demotivating. It is essential that flexibility is maintained, both in terms of the documentation used and those involved with implementing and supporting the process.

■ A pilot project in advance of committing fully to NVQs was extremely valuable in terms of understanding the issues and gaining experience.

DERBY COLLEGE: WILMORTON LIBRARY

—— 7 ——

Preparing the Organisation or Department

COLLECTING INFORMATION ON NVQs

Once you have established the nature of the competence-based standards you are going to introduce, you are ready to consider the implications of their introduction.

If you are also introducing NVQs (with national standards as their base) you will be ready to collect information on these qualifications from the awarding bodies, which may include the relevant ILB itself (see Chapter 1).

Each NVQ will have specific requirements attached relating to the assessment process. For example, some NVQs have a requirement for workplace assessors to be 'registered' or licensed. Some may supply documentation for recording assessment as part of the initial registration fee. Check on the costs of such materials. You do *not* have to use these (see Fletcher 1997c and NCVQ 1997).

You may be introducing a full NVQ (ie, all units of a specified qualification) or units of more than one full NVQ, but all NVQs will include arrangements for quality control – referred to as 'verification' or 'moderation'. An *internal* verifier is a designated person within the company who monitors the work of in-company assessors (often supervisors or first-line managers). An *external* verifier is an awarding body representative who will visit a sample of companies on a regular basis to ensure that standards are being maintained and that the assessment system is operating as it should.

The costs of verification are often built into the NVQ operational system. They may be included in an initial registration fee, or in annual operating costs. You should ask for clarification of all costs involved.

'Certification' refers to the award of certificates to successful candidates. This usually involves a separate fee and can be charged on a unit certificate basis (usually around £10 per unit), or on a full NVQ basis (usually between £35 and £125 per certificate). You should clarify whether fees include issue of an NVQ certificate. Awarding bodies have their own system of charging for their own certificates, and the NCVQ also has a certification charge.

What to ask about NVQs

- What are the requirements for assessment of units?
- Are there specific requirements for
  - training of assessors?
  - registration of assessors?
  - costs?
- Is there an initial registration fee?
- If so, what does this registration fee cover?
- Is the registration fee payable annually?
- Is there an 'assessment centre approval process' attached to registration? Does this meet the requirements of the Common Accord?
- What are verification and moderation arrangements?
- Are there any hidden costs involved?
- What are the arrangements for certification of successful candidates?
- What are the certification fees?
- Is there any separate arrangement for assessment of knowledge and understanding?
- Is there a procedure for accreditation of prior learning?

CONSIDER THE IMPLICATIONS IN OPERATIONAL TERMS

Introducing competence-based standards and NVQs will have a direct impact on the training culture within your organisation.

Systems of workplace assessment require commitment and involvement. Learning programmes will need to be revised or developed to contribute towards achievement of required standards. Staff will take on new roles and responsibilities – a point to note when discussing changes with trade unions.

You might think of the introduction of competence-based standards and NVQs as a programme for change. Like all change programmes, it will require careful planning to ensure that the staff resources and expertise are available, and that the new actions for change will influence company operations only in a positive sense.

You will need to establish an in-company assessment model. This means considering who will be designated assessors and how they will assess. Who will train assessors and how will they be trained? What costs are involved in this activity? Does the awarding body or ILB specify a training programme or can you develop one of your own? Will your assessors gain qualifications in assessment? Is this a requirement?

You must also consider *quality control*. Who will be designated as internal verifier? Who will be the key contact for introducing standards and NVQs? Who will liaise with awarding bodies regarding external verification and certification?

You will also need to consider training implications. Who will be responsible for ensuring that training contributes to achievement of standards? When will training programmes be developed? How will training delivery be affected?

If this sounds like a great deal of work – it is! Any programme for change requires considerable effort and it is essential that all roles and responsibilities are clarified before implementation begins.

The checklists below will help you with some of the key questions you need to consider at this vital planning stage.

Introducing standards and NVQs – initial checklist

Does your organisation have

- a clear training policy?
- a clear training strategy?
- a plan for implementing standards and NVQs?
- a senior staff member designated with responsibility for implementation?
- job descriptions which outline training responsibilities?
- a staff appraisal system?
- a system for forecasting staffing needs?
- an agreed culture?
- existing company qualifications?
- existing reward/incentive schemes?
- existing arrangements with awarding bodies/educational institutions for award of qualifications?

- existing continuous assessment schemes?
- company-defined learning/training programmes?
- company-defined standards?
- selection/recruitment policies linked to job descriptions?

All or any of the above activities can influence, or be influenced by, the introduction of competence-based standards and NVQs. In order to understand the implications and benefits of each activity, you must have a clear understanding of the concepts and principles of these new developments, and of the specific operational requirements of the NVQs you intend to introduce.

If you decide you need help to plan the introduction of standards and NVQs, ILBs and awarding bodies can provide guidance. Consultancy help is also available, but make sure you check that your chosen source of help is fully cognisant of developments and is able to consider the application of these developments within your specific company context.

Introducing standards and NVQs – staff role checklist

Management responsibility
Who is responsible for

- implementing standards/NVQs at
  - organisational level?
  - departmental level?
- liaison with awarding bodies?
- monitoring effectiveness of new systems?
- arranging development of competence-based training programmes?

Operational responsibility
Who is responsible for

- initial assessment procedures (including assessment of prior learning)?
- assessing candidates' performance at work and recording assessment?
- monitoring (verifying) assessors' work including countersigning assessments?
- identifying training needs?
- preparing training plans?

Trade unions

A brief note regarding discussions with trade unions is essential. By now, you are probably fully aware that the introduction of competence-based standards and NVQs can have far-reaching implications and benefits for your organisation.

Not least of these is the potential perceived change in staff roles and responsibilities. For those companies which have introduced total quality management, or ISO 9000, or some form of total quality system, the idea of line management's greater involvement in the development and assessment of staff will not come as any great shock. In fact, competence-based standards should serve to make explicit what supervisors and line managers are doing on a daily basis anyway – continuously assessing the performance of staff for whom they have direct responsibility.

However, the introduction of assessment recording systems, on an individual basis, is likely to be met by a wide range of reactions that you must be prepared to deal with. No doubt trade unions will want to question the changes in roles and responsibilities – the introduction of NVQs, with external recognition for work performance, is a form of reward or incentive system.

Some of the issues which may arise will relate to existing incentive schemes (or previous ones). Others may relate to the fact that assessors are being given responsibility for 'signing off competence'. This latter issue may be particularly problematic in sectors where health and safety is a key issue. For example, what happens if a line manager/supervisor 'signs off' an employee as competent in installing a delicate or potentially dangerous piece of equipment and something goes wrong with that equipment?

This will be a valid and pertinent point to be addressed in many industries, as will issues pertaining to incentive and reward. But there is no universal guidance on these matters. Careful planning through consideration of all the issues outlined in this and the previous chapter will help you prepare for such discussions.

Accreditation of prior learning

The accreditation of prior learning (APL) permits the award of credit towards a qualification on the basis of evidence drawn from an individual's past achievements. For companies, this means that you can use the APL assessment process to take a competence audit of your staff and provide them with credit towards an NVQ as recognition of their current level of competence.

An additional benefit for you is that, having completed this assessment, training needs will have been clearly identified, on both individual and group bases, and future training can be targeted to those areas where it is really needed. This will obviously save time and provide a more cost-effective training solution as well as providing motivation for staff to be both assessed and trained.

The major awarding bodies have developed and agreed policies for the operation of APL in connection with a wide range of qualifications. However, procedures for operating the APL process within all occupational areas have not yet been finalised. You will therefore need to check that procedures are in place within the relevant occupational areas.

The costs involved will include a fee for verification (paid to the awarding body) and training of assessors. Given the overall benefits of operating APL as an initial assessment process, this is a cost-effective means of introducing NVQs.

Once again, should you need help to introduce APL, check that your source of help is fully cognisant with the concepts, principles and operational requirements involved. Avoid paper-led portfolio systems (see Fletcher 1997c).

Part III

Implementing Your System

8

Staff Briefing and Development

STAFF BRIEFING

Once you have a plan for the introduction of competence-based standards and NVQs, you need to consider how to communicate those plans to everyone involved. If you are using Investors in People as a development process, the communication system you prepare will be business-led and incorporate NVQs as one component of change.

Much will depend upon your implementation plan, but it is usually a good idea to consider an organisational briefing which outlines the reasons behind the decision to introduce new developments, together with the benefits to both the organisation and the individual.

You might consider using an existing staff newsletter, or networking structures to cascade information. Alternatively, a special staff briefing might be arranged. Whatever your choice, consider the following points for inclusion in a major briefing exercise:

- reasons why standards and NVQs are being introduced
- explanation of what standards and NVQs are
- description of areas they are being introduced in
- details of the order they are being introduced – and why
- how the company will benefit from the introduction
- how individuals will benefit from the introduction
- trade union support
- what the introduction means in terms of staff roles and responsibilities
- when the first implementation will start
- how it will be monitored

- procedures for people to communicate ideas and feedback
- request for applications for first candidates (if you are conducting a pilot scheme first).

Staff development

Companies have been quick to realise the potential flexibility that competence-based standards offer to the training function. With explicit and measurable standards of expected performance which can be made available to everyone who uses them, the design and delivery of training becomes less hit or miss and more directly targeted to individual and group and company needs.

However, as companies begin to introduce new competence-based standards and NVQs, they are also beginning to realise the importance of staff development, particularly for assessors.

Most of us have a particular perception of assessment. The traditional view was outlined in Part I. If you are unclear about the principles and concepts of competence-based assessment, and how they differ from the more traditional approach, you should read through Chapter 5 before continuing with this section.

NVQ assessment model

All NVQs operate within a defined assessment model (see Figure 8.1). Assessment is determined by the elements of competence, range statements and performance criteria which form the standards of competence. Assessment itself is a process of obtaining evidence and making judgements about that evidence.

The key form of assessment within NVQs is therefore observation of performance. However, this is not always possible, particularly in the case of various contingencies or hazardous environments.

Assessors operating within competence-based systems must therefore be fully aware of various methods of assessment and their use within the workplace if they are to assess the full specified range of activities.

ASSESSOR TRAINING

One particular danger of introducing competence-based standards and NVQs is the tendency to assume that people already know about assessment. After all, isn't competence-based assessment only making explicit what supervisors and line managers do anyway?

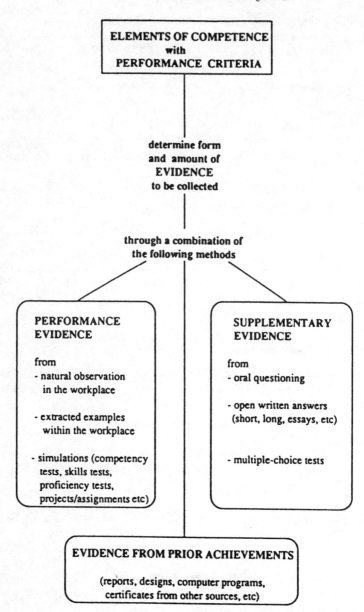

Figure 8.1 The NVQ assessment model

This is true, although perhaps it would be more accurate to say that competence-based assessment makes explicit what supervisors and line managers *should* be doing anyway! How consistent is continuous assessment in your organisation? How good are your line managers at recognising and reporting training needs, or completing annual appraisals?

While we may all have a good idea of what assessment is, when it comes to actually doing it we find that our ideas are not the same as those held by the people we have to assess, or by our colleagues who have to conduct a similar assessment.

The point of introducing competence-based systems is to gain *consistency*. Consistent maintenance of standards, both in performance and assessment, can contribute to development of performance. It is important to recognise, therefore, that *training of workplace assessors* is vital to the successful implementation and operation of competence-based systems. Quality assurance requirements now include a demand that assessors and verifiers achieve national accreditation.

Training programmes for assessors

Workplace assessors need to be competent in their assessment role. You may find that the awarding bodies for the NVQs which you plan to introduce offer assessor-training programmes. The benefits of these are that they are usually sector-specific and deal with issues arising from the particular NVQ.

However, with a focus on quality of assessors, you should check that the assessor training will meet your operational requirements and national criteria for approval when accredited and that it includes the following:

- basic concepts of competence-based assessment
- issues of evidence of competence
- assessor skills, including use of various methods of assessment
- maintaining quality of assessment
- procedures and processes for assessment of performance and for assessment of knowledge and understanding (these are sometimes separate, eg, the financial services sector)
- procedures for accreditation of prior learning, including issues of evidence from past achievements
- verification/moderation procedures
- recording procedures and documentation (tailored to meet *your* needs)

- certification procedures
- appeals procedures.

You may find that the content or the duration of assessor training courses on offer do not meet your operational needs. You may choose to develop and deliver your own in-company programme, or to use external consultants to do this for you. Various open learning packages are also available. Once again, the issue of making sure that your selected consultant is *au fait* with developments and key concepts is a paramount issue.

CERTIFICATION FOR ASSESSORS

Awarding bodies have overall responsibility for assessment in connection with NVQs because they award the final certificates. You might therefore find requirements for 'registration' of assessors. There will also be a requirement for assessors to achieve a recognised qualification. You can arrange this through liaison with an awarding body (or your external consultant could take care of this for you). This will, of course, involve your in-company assessors undergoing assessment. (The terminology gets confusing – who assesses assessors?)

This need not be complicated. All your in-company assessors will be monitored by an internal and an external verifier (see p. 58 for explanations of these terms). Assessors will therefore be demonstrating competence in their assessment role on an ongoing basis – in the same way as the people they are assessing are demonstrating competence in their work roles. Assistance with funding for this development is available from Training and Enterprise Councils.

INTERNAL VERIFIER TRAINING

Internal verifiers are in-company staff responsible for monitoring assessment. They may also have a role as 'countersigning officers' – responsible for signing the assessment documentation to support the decision of the first-line assessor. Verifiers will need to understand the basic concepts, principles and procedures of competence-based assessment in the same depth as first-line assessors. They will also need to be clear about the verifier's role and liaison with awarding bodies.

Accreditation of prior learning (APL)

Once again, a separate note on this issue, although it is an integral part of competence-based assessment.

If you are planning to introduce APL, you will have included training in this form of assessment in your initial assessor training package. It is essential to the credibility of the assessment system that assessors are aware of issues relating to evidence from past achievements and can provide quality guidance to candidates.

A question of choice

When introducing competence-based standards and NVQs, your company can choose whether to use nationally agreed standards of competence as they stand, or to enhance or 'contextualise' them to meet organisational demands. Similarly, you can choose to make use of the assessor training packages available to you or to develop your own. These decisions must be based on a review of the specific NVQs you plan to introduce.

— 9 —

Starting, Maintaining and Expanding the System

PILOT FIRST CANDIDATES AND ASSESSORS

When your initial training programmes are complete, you are ready to start your first assessments. Remember, these are not traditional assessment procedures of a one-off nature: your in-company assessment scheme will operate on a continuous day-by-day basis.

Briefing the candidates

All candidates for assessment should be fully briefed about the assessment system. They should have easy access to the standards at all times – and to their assessor.

The designated assessor (usually a line manager), who may be responsible for several candidates (usually his or her own staff), should meet with the candidate and ensure that a clear *assessment plan is agreed*.

Assessment plans

The purpose of an assessment plan is to set parameters for both candidate and assessor. Both need to be clear on *what* is being assessed and *how* it is being assessed.

As competence-based assessment focuses on evidence of performance, assessor and candidate can decide what forms of evidence are most likely to be created in the normal work pattern of the candidate.

The assessor and candidate will need to agree which *units of competence* the candidate will be aiming to achieve. They can also agree a timescale for assessment. Figure 9.1 illustrates a typical process for

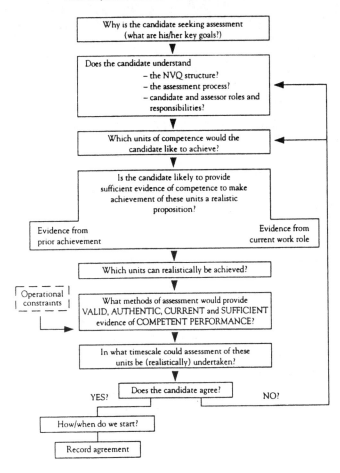

Figure 9.1 A typical assessment plan process

agreeing an assessment plan. Such a plan will be a requirement if you are seeking funding from TECs to assist with your implementation.

Assessor support

Assessors will need support, not only to help them in the role, but also to ensure that standards are maintained. A networking system, allowing assessors to meet on a regular basis, would enable a forum for exchange of ideas and mutual support to be established.

Regular meetings with internal verifiers and external verifiers should also be encouraged. These arrangements will obviously need to fit in with operational requirements, but the importance of assessor support to general maintenance of a quality assessment system should not be underestimated.

OPERATE RECORDING SYSTEMS

There is no reason why you cannot operate your own recording system, particularly if you find that the one offered by the awarding body(ies) does not meet your day-to-day operational needs. However, you should ensure that any recording system includes clear guidance for assessors (as a general reference point) and also allows sufficient space for recording of evidence presented, and signatures of assessor, verifier and candidate.

Documentation relating to assessment must be kept up to date and available for verifiers to review. Assessment documentation and evidence collected can be used for final assessment, particularly where evidence from past achievement is included. Any collection of evidence by a single candidate can be compiled into a 'portfolio' which serves as an assessment document in itself. However, a portfolio is *not* a mandatory requirement.

The assessor is responsible for recording the results of assessment. Records should be maintained legibly and accurately and be accessible to candidate, assessor, assessor-colleagues and verifiers. However, confidentiality between candidate and those staff with legitimate access to records must be maintained. For help on designing and implementing non-bureaucratic assessment recording systems see Fletcher (1997c).

MONITOR PROCEDURES AND PROGRESS

The internal and external verifiers will be responsible for monitoring of the assessors and the assessment system. However, maintenance of standards is a key issue for your company – consistency of performance through the introduction of standards is one of the key reasons for introducing competence-based standards.

You may wish to introduce your own monitoring system, perhaps using the external verifier as a source of information, as he or she will have a general overview of the progress of a number of candidates and a number of assessors.

Specific questions you may consider include:

- How is the assessor:candidate ratio working out?
- Are assessors able to cope with the number of candidates?
- Are assessors/candidates having any difficulties with
  - types of evidence required?
  - organisation of workload to produce the range of evidence required?
  - coping with assessment documentation?

In addition to monitoring the actual assessment system, you will also want to consider measures of effectiveness as the first part of your evaluation of the new system's contribution to improved performance.

The measures you may choose to use in this respect will be similar to those used to evaluate the effectiveness of training:

- increased productivity
- lower absenteeism
- lower level of complaints
- decreased reject rate.

It is probably a good idea to begin compiling your overall evaluation plan at this stage. By using initial information on progress you will begin to formulate a clear idea of the most appropriate measures to apply.

PLAN FOR EXPANSION

When your pilot programme is running smoothly, you will need to consider plans for expansion. The following questions might be considered:

- How many more candidates for assessment do we have in this occupational area?
- Do we have adequate numbers of assessors?
- How can we phase training of assessors and introduction of assessment across all staff in this occupational area?
- What will be the next occupational area in which we will introduce NVQs?
- Are there any differences between operational requirements for NVQs in the second occupational area?
- What difficulties have arisen in this first area that we can also foresee in the next?

- What solutions have we tried/have worked/can we forecast for new areas?

Importance of maintaining standards

As we have already noted on several occasions in these last few chapters, perhaps the biggest benefit for companies introducing competence-based standards and assessment is the potential for *consistency* of performance.

Achieving consistency requires commitment – commitment to effective training and to quality control. All of this requires time and effort on the part of everyone involved.

Most companies have found that the early stages of introduction throw up a range of difficulties, mainly because people are attempting to adjust not only to a new way of working but also to a new way of *thinking*.

Focusing on performance, and on the *outcomes of performance*, requires a shift in thinking. Using new forms of assessment, developing new skills, and taking responsibility for new forms of record keeping all involve a 'learning curve'. Results will not be immediate and no doubt there will be complaints of 'time wasting record keeping' and 'irrelevance' during the first few months.

Getting help

The following information section provides an outline of the operation of Training and Enterprise Councils (TECs) – one source of help for introducing and/or expanding NVQ operation in your company.

INFORMATION SECTION

What are TECs and why do they exist?

It was a White Paper, *Employment for the 1990s* (HMSO 1988) which proposed the establishment of Training and Enterprise Councils (TECs) in England and Wales and Local Enterprise Councils (LECs) in Scotland. The timescale for this new development was made clear: 'The Government expect that a national network of TECs will evolve gradually over a period of three to four years'. The philosophy behind this proposal was that:

each community must shape a clear vision stretching beyond existing programmes, organisation and methods of delivery. It must place education, training and enterprise in the broader context of economic and industrial development

The establishment of TECs and LECs was based on five major principles of reform:

- A locally based system.
- An employer-led partnership.
- A focused approach.
- An accent on performance.
- An enterprise organisation.
  (Employment Department, 1990)

It was envisaged that the first prospective TECs would enter their development phases in July 1989 and a transition to full TEC operation would occur in April 1990, with up to 60 TECs operational or ready to become operational by July 1990.

The funding provided for TEC expenditure on the development phase was initially limited to £11 million. The overall management, control and direction of work associated with TECs rested with the Director General of the Training Agency, who was supported by a formal Project Board. Action Managers were appointed with responsibility for coordinating, monitoring and reporting on each block of work involved in the TEC Project. Issue Managers were also appointed and were responsible for delivery of particular products or outputs. Project Management Guidelines were issued and the Project Management Unit managed progress reports.

TECs are independent companies, each having a contract with the Secretary of State for Education and Employment. They are normally limited by guarantee and run by a Board of Directors. (The original requirement, as stated in the prospectus (Employment Department 1993), was that two-thirds of their boards would be private sector employers at Chief Executive or Managing Director level, the rest being drawn from leaders of education, economic development, trade unions, voluntary organisations and the public sector.) The key focus was that they should be run by business leaders and aim to provide the country with the skilled and enterprising workforce needed for sustained growth and prosperity. By the end of 1992 (last available figures) it was estimated that 1085 businesses and community leaders were involved with TECs in England.

The TEC Project, led by the Training Agency, aimed to coordinate the planning, management and delivery of TEC implementation. The scope of the Project included all efforts associated with establishing:

- a full network of operational TECs in England and Wales with appropriate support arrangements
- a platform for the growth of TEC responsibilities towards a role for TECs at the heart of local economic development.

The Training Agency established a Project Management Unit to take forward this planning and implementation. The TECs were set Strategic Priorities (which have not changed). Since these were set, quantitative measures have been clarified in terms of the National Education and Training Targets.

TEC/LEC STRATEGIC PRIORITIES

- Encourage effective employer investment in skills, and stimulate employers to meet the lifetime learning targets.
- Help young people achieve their full potential, and raise attainment in line with the foundation learning targets.
- Stimulate individuals to take responsibility for their own development, and so contribute to achieving lifetime learning targets.
- Help unemployed people and those at a disadvantage in the jobs market to get back to work and to develop their abilities to the full.
- Stimulate the provision of high quality and flexible education and training, in support of the National Targets.
- Encourage enterprise throughout the economy, particularly through the continued growth of small business and self-employment.

In *Training and Enterprise, Priorities for Action* (Training Agency 1989), the Aims and Priorities for TECs were detailed:

- to help businesses improve their performance by encouraging them to plan and undertake training to achieve clear business aims
- to help ensure that young people acquire the skills the economy needs
- to help ensure that unemployed people, and particularly the long-term unemployed, acquire the skills, experience and enterprise to help them find and keep a job
- to encourage new businesses to start and existing businesses to grow
- to help make the providers of vocational education aware of local

labour market needs and to promote links between education and employers
- to improve the training system by ensuring that there is an effective local, sectoral and national framework.

These aims and priorities related to the first TECs, to Industry Training Organisations, to Local Enterprise Agencies and to the Employment Department Training Agency. Underpinning all aims and priorities was a commitment to continue to promote equal access to training and enterprise for people at a disadvantage in the labour market.

NATIONAL EDUCATION AND TRAINING TARGETS

Foundation learning

- By 1997, 80 per cent of young people to reach NVQ Level II or equivalent.
- Training and education to NVQ Level III (or equivalent) available to all young people who can benefit.
- By 2000, 50 per cent of young people to reach NVQ Level III (or equivalent).
- Education and training provision to develop self-reliance, flexibility and breadth.

Lifetime learning

- By 1996, all employees should take part in training or development activities as the norm.
- By 1996, at least half of the employed workforce should be aiming for qualifications or units towards them within the NVQ system, preferably in the context of individual action plans and with support from employers.
- By 2000, 50 per cent of the employed workforce should be qualified to NVQ or its academic equivalent as a minimum.
- By 1996, at least half of the medium-sized and larger organisations should qualify as Investors in People, assessed by the relevant TEC.

(Specific details of initiatives such as Investors in People can be found in other sections of this book.)

HOW DO TECS OPERATE?

There are now 82 TECs/LECs. The geographic areas covered by individual TECs vary. Each TEC, during its development phase, prepared a Corporate Plan to provide a basis for its operations. These plans also included information about the geographical area to be covered as well as the extent of support from the local community and priorities for change and improvement in the local labour market.

Each TEC Corporate Plan uses a market assessment as its basis – this includes a review of long- and short-term needs of businesses and individuals. The Plan includes a mission statement, three-year strategic objectives, a framework for action, a business plan and an operational structure.

As always, the operation of TECs must have control arrangements which strike the right balance between local autonomy for TECs and central accountability for public funds. A total of £1.4 billion was spent on Department of Employment funded training, enterprise and education programmes during 1991/2 while the network of TECs was developing – the network of 82 TECs was completed in October 1991 (see Figure 9.2). The first TECs/LECs to become operational were Calderdale/Kirklees, Hertfordshire and Thames Valley Enterprise, all beginning in April 1990. The London TECs were the last to be established, each covering a specific area of London, during August to October 1991.

TEC PERFORMANCE

Since the establishment of the TECs and LECs, greater importance has been placed on measurable outputs. During 1991/2, 25 per cent of payments for the two biggest programmes (Youth Training and Employment Training) were based on achievements in terms of qualifications gained by trainees and job placements for Employment Training. This was an improvement on the 10 per cent figure for 1990/91. It is estimated that the figure for 1993 will vary between 25 per cent and 40 per cent.

Performance-related funding also exists for achievement in specified areas. Targets set for 1991/2 included:

■ The number of people obtaining a National Vocational Qualification (NVQ) level II or above (level I for Special Training Needs Category

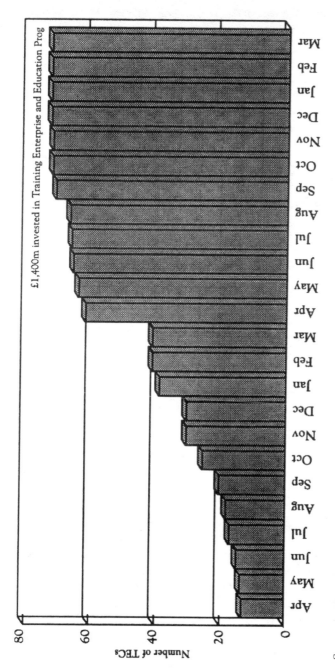

Source: TEC Achievements & Plans System (TECAPS) & TEC Invoice
Reproduced in TECS 1992 (Employment Dept 1993)

Figure 9.2 Growth of TEC network

B) and a job, self-employment or Enterprise Allowance Scheme (EAS) on leaving Youth Training.

- The number of long-term unemployed people (two years or more unemployed on entry) who have jobs, are self-employed or entered EAS three months after Employment Training.
- The number of YT and ET ethnic minority trainees who have jobs, are self-employed or entered EAS on leaving training (YT) or three months after training (ET).
- The number of trainees with disabilities on YT and ET securing jobs, self-employment or entering EAS on leaving training (YT) or three months after leaving training (ET).
- The number of YT and ET trainees resident in special areas, or other appropriate group, who secure jobs, self-employment or enter EAS on leaving training (YT) or three months after training (ET).

In 1991/2 performance-related awards worth over £27 million were made to TECs where targets were achieved. For 1992, the priorities were stated as:

- ethnic minority trainees
- inner cities and special geographic areas
- trainees with disabilities
- Investors in People commitments
- education developments.

TECs and LECs have been involved in a number of national initiatives since their inception. These include Gateways, Access to Assessment, Skillchoice, Investors in People and, of course, NVQs. All of these initiatives have attempted to support a particular aspect of change.

With each new initiative, TECs are provided with a 'Consultative Document' and then a 'Prospectus'. TECs, as independent companies, decide whether to bid for the funding available to take forward these initiatives; thus different TECs will be operating different initiatives at different times. For example, the Access to Assessment initiative was, in 1993, in its third year, while Skillchoice only began in April of that year.

There is a growing awareness that TECs need to integrate the various services and products they offer, and to provide more of a business focus with an understanding of business needs. Much attention has been given to the individual, with marketing and promotion directed through TEC networks of 'providers' – still mainly colleges. However, the greater emphasis on performance targets, with funding being linked to the achievement of greater numbers achieving qualifications (see National

Targets and Performance above), has led to an acknowledgement that marketing to employers will yield better and faster results.

Perhaps this is also a recognition that a qualification, or part of a qualification, for work will only be of real value to any individual when it is also valued by the employer whom they hope it will impress.

— 10 —

Making the Most of the New Standards

10.1 INTRODUCTION

This chapter looks briefly at ways in which new competence-based standards can be used as a basis for a range of organisational planning and monitoring functions. Rather than presenting an ideal model it raises questions and suggests issues which need to be addressed. Indeed, there can be no ideal model – one of the basic concepts underlying the new forms of competence-based standards is their potential for *flexibility*. To suggest a model for their use would therefore be counter-productive.

If you keep in mind the key points – standards are *outcome-based* and assessment is about collecting *evidence of actual performance* – then you will be able to apply the real potential of competence-based approaches to your own organisational needs. Expansion of the ideas expressed here can be found in Fletcher 1993 and 1997c.

10.2 STANDARDS AND ORGANISATIONAL DEVELOPMENT

Implementing a new form of standards which are explicit and measurable gives you the chance to consider and formalise market information and assess how you can capitalise on the opportunities (and minimise constraints) in current and future market scenarios.

Market opportunities in which implementation of standards can probably be most beneficial include:

- need for consistency in quality

- growth in the industry or sector
- introduction of new legislation
- introduction of technological change
- deregulation and competition
- raising of public image of the organisation.

Constraints on the introduction of standards include:

- lack of resources
- complexity and size of task
- lack of management support
- fragmented sector (which delays standards development anyway).

When planning the evaluation of the introduction of competence-based standards and NVQs in relation to organisation development, the following checklist may be useful:

- What were the key objectives in implementing standards?
- What were the priority objectives?
- What were the objectives in each occupation area?
- What milestones to achievement of objectives have been identified?
- What are the resource implications?
- What actions have had the most impact on acceptance of standards within the company?
- What actions/issues have had the most impact on rejection of standards within the company?

10.3 EXPANDING THE USE OF STANDARDS

Once standards are in place for assessment of workplace performance and for achievement of NVQs, you will be ready to consider their use in other areas of organisational activity.

Your choice of activities, and their priority ordering, will depend very much upon your current organisational structure, and the administrative, managerial and communication systems currently in place.

Standards may be used effectively in the following areas:

- performance appraisal
- manpower planning
- selection and recruitment
- multiskilling

- revision of job descriptions/functions
- training and development.

Standards can also be updated to incorporate changes within the organisation, including the introduction of new technology or re-organisation.

10.4 AN ACTION PLAN

When considering how to expand the use of standards within your organisation, you will need to establish a clear action plan.

Key questions you may consider will include:

- What needs to be done to achieve the introduction of standards for every employee within the organisation?
- Who is going to be responsible for implementation activities?
- In which key areas will we utilise standards (see list above)?
- How long will it take?
- How much will it cost?
- What are our priorities?
- How will we measure progress?

Your action plan may be structured as follows:

- purpose of document
- key objectives, priorities, actions, issues
- personnel resources and management structure
- finances
- standards in use (percentage of workforce)
- standards under development
- timescale
- evaluation
- implementation plan in each area of development.

10.5 STANDARDS AND PERFORMANCE APPRAISAL

If you are already using standards in continuous assessment of work-place performance (ie, with NVQs), the expansion to a performance appraisal system will not be too difficult.

You may treat the ongoing assessment as 'formative' evidence and link this to the annual performance appraisal. There are one or two points to bear in mind in this connection, however.

First, you should avoid making the annual performance appraisal a 'summative' assessment which leads directly to award of NVQs or the units which constitute them. This would encourage a 'time-serving' basis for awards which runs counter to the aims of NVQs – individuals should have access to awards on the basis of their individual performance.

Second, you must consider how such systems will be perceived by those who use them. Assessment for NVQs is directly linked to an incentive/reward system – external recognition through qualification. Performance appraisal is often linked to promotion or merit bonus or salary structure.

You need to be clear how you plan to link the two kinds of assessment. If people achieve NVQs, does this lead automatically to promotion, or salary increase, or merit bonus? What will be the key purpose of the performance appraisal system? Is it a completely 'open' reporting system? Are 'promotion markings' or any part of the report kept secret from the individual? (It is to be hoped that most systems have moved on from this practice.)

When considering the use of competence-based standards in performance appraisal, therefore, you must also consider how your appraisal system links with ongoing assessment of workplace performance and also with any other incentive or reward systems which you currently (or are planning to) operate.

Establishing the performance appraisal system, once your objectives are clear, involves a process of utilising the competence-based standards in a format that will facilitate an annual feedback and review.

If assessment has been continuous throughout the year, then feedback at an appointed annual time should not come as any surprise. The appraisal interview will present a good opportunity for training needs to be clearly identified and agreed, together with a development plan, as well as establishing objectives for the next year. The explicit nature of competence-based standards will provide a sound basis for discussion, as will the requirement for evidence of performance. In short, the nature and purpose of performance appraisal need not change, but the basis for discussion can be more explicit and based on clearer forms of evidence of the past year's performance.

Figure 10.1 (page 107), taken from Gerald Randell's *Staff Appraisal* (Randell 1984), may be a helpful guide in considering the *functions* of performance appraisal in your organisation. Once you are clear on the specific functions that are applicable to your existing, or planned, scheme you can consider how best to utilise competence-based standards in this area.

10.6 STANDARDS AND MANPOWER PLANNING

Manpower planning is the systematic analysis of the company's resources, the construction of a forecast of its future manpower requirements from this base, with special concentration on the efficient use of manpower at both these stages, and the planning necessary to ensure that the manpower supply will match the forecast requirement.

Put more simply: *manpower planning is ensuring that the right number of people are in the right place at the right time.*

When looking forward for your manpower needs, what current measures do you use? How clear are your future plans? How much do you know about the roles that people carry out in your organisation and the actual skills they need; or what new skills will be needed to cope with planned change?

These have always been the difficult questions faced by those responsible for considering the future needs of an organisation. Manpower planning has become a complex and sophisticated activity with computer models and mathematical techniques being used in forecasting. Competence-based standards are not going to solve these problems, but because of their explicit nature they can contribute to the more effective identification of skills and knowledge required in new work roles.

Manpower planning is really a series of activities:

- analysis of current resources
- forecasting of future needs
- planning to supply these needs.

The activities of analysing current resources and forecasting future needs relate directly to the performance required. In turn, the performance required relates directly to skills and knowledge expected of employees.

If performance is monitored on a continuous basis, and the results of this performance measurement collated as part of your evaluation exercise, you will have valuable data to inform your future plans.

The purposes of an appraisal scheme are:

- to assess future potential
- to assess training and development needs
- to assess past performance
- to establish control of behaviour
- to bring about changes in behaviour
- to help improve current performance.

The main steps of exercising management control are:

- setting standards
- monitoring performance
- comparing performance with the standard
- taking action that may be needed (either to improve the performance or to change the standards).

The main intentions of an appraisal scheme are:

- *Evaluation*, to enable to organisation to share out money, promotions and perquisites (perks) apparently fairly
- *Auditing*, to discover the work potential, both present and future, of individuals and departments
- *Constructing succession plans* for manpower, departmental and corporate planning
- *Discovering training needs* by exposing inadequacies and deficiencies which could be remedied by training
- *Motivating staff* to reach organisational standards and objectives
- *Developing individuals* by advice, information and attempts at shaping their behaviour by praise or punishment
- *Checking the effectiveness* of personnel procedures and practices.

Source: Gerald Randell, *Staff Appraisal* (1984)

Figure 10.1 The functions of performance appraisal

10.7 STANDARDS, SELECTION AND RECRUITMENT

This section also incorporates the use of standards in the revision of job descriptions and functions.

Recruitment and selection is about choosing staff. Again this involves a number of activities:

Deciding what → Casting the → Shortlisting → Decision-
the job needs   recruitment   making
                net

Staff selection may often be a process conducted by gut feeling, despite training of managers and personnel staff in a wide range of techniques. The use of clearly defined standards can help to develop this gut feeling approach into a more informed and informative one, for both the interviewer and the interviewee.

Let's take the first activity – *deciding what the job needs.*

If competence-based standards have been introduced, then the expectations of the job someone undertakes will be clearly defined in terms of standards or expectations of performance. These standards will include the skills and knowledge required, and a specified range of activities in which performance must be undertaken.

This then, will provide a basis on which a job specification and person specification can be devised.

In *casting the recruitment net* you may wish to consider which competence-based qualifications would provide evidence of the performance level you are seeking. In particular, there may be specific units of competence which may up the specification you have developed.

You can consider whether you need someone who has attained all the relevant units, or whether you are prepared to take someone who has *some* of them, requiring you to arrange training in those remaining.

This consideration of NVQs held by prospective candidates may be more a consideration for the future – NVQs are as yet fairly new and it will take some time for their full use in the labour market to be established. However, the exercise of planning by units of competence does help to focus your mind, and the minds of the prospective employees, on the issue of evidence of performance. This approach will contribute to your *shortlisting* and *decision-making* exercises. What evidence can candidates supply of their current level of expertise? How valid is that evidence?

You may even want to consider establishing an initial assessment for interviewees, or asking them to present what they feel is valid evidence of their current level of performance.

10.8 STANDARDS AND MULTISKILLING

Because the process of 'multiskilling' involves looking at the transferability of skills and the relationship between various activities within an organisational structure, competence-based standards are of particular help in this area.

You will recall from Part I that competence-based standards are derived through the process of *functional* analysis. A focus on functions rather than tasks contributes to a broader view of competence and incorporates aspects of task and contingency management as well as operating within the working environment.

This functional basis of standards can be used to facilitate your analysis and planning of multiskilling activities. ILBs may even be able to supply you with details of the original functional analysis which led to the derivation of competence-based standards. Alternatively, a good external consultant who has worked on competence-based developments will be able to assist you.

An overview of the sectoral standards, particularly at the higher levels of 'key work roles' (from which units of competence are derived) will also give you valuable information.

The following case study outlines work of the UK Learning Organisations Network – a group of UK companies which have been working together to define competencies for change agents. Note the use of the word *competencies* and not *competences* – the latter being the UK (NVQ) style of competence-based standard.

The case study gives readers a look at alternative approaches to the development and introduction of a competence-based approach.

It focuses on one role within organisations and has yet to approach the difficult problem of rigour of assessment, but clearly demonstrates how a definite link between a competence-based system and business needs is a key requirement for any organisation.

■ CASE STUDY ■

Change Agent Competencies
UK Learning Organisations Network*

The following case study, kindly provided by Time Manager International, shows how a set of change agent competencies has been developed by member organisations of the UK Learning Organisation Network. The case study also illustrates three issues:

- an initial networking process where generic competencies can be devised to suit the strategic human resource requirements of a broad range of commercial and non-commercial organisations
- how competence development can be driven by practical business requirements
- that competence development can be relatively inexpensive if driven by partner organisations which have a clear vision of what they are trying to achieve.

The Learning Organisation Network

The Learning Organisation Network is an informal group of private and public sector organisations which have demonstrated their commitment to the concept of the Learning Organisation. Member organisations include Rover, Digital Equipment, Midland Bank, Sainsburys, Time Manager International, Lucas, Rank Xerox, Milton Keynes College, the NHS and Royal Mail.

The Group first met in London in November 1992, following an initiative from Rover, Digital Equipment and the RSA with support from the HRD Partnership. A second meeting was held in April 1993 at Rover where Barrie Oxtoby from the Rover Learning Business shared the work that Rover had done in developing a range of change agent competencies. Members of the Group saw the value of this work and a team, coordinated by Ron Dillion, then Training Quality Assurance Manager at Rank Xerox, was formed to take it further.

The vision

The vision of the Network at this time was to devise a set of change agent competencies that:

* Written and compiled by Gary Ling of Time Manager International.

- were relevant, credible and conceptually sound
- were sufficiently flexible to support the specific requirements of individual member companies
- recognised what people had already done
- potentially formed the basis of future development activity
- facilitated a self-assessment process that could be effectively and speedily validated
- allowed people who do not see themselves as change agents to recognise that they are.

Once the competencies had been developed, the role of the network was envisaged as being similar to that of an awarding body. In a less structured way, then, for example, the awarding of NVQs, members nominated individuals within their organisations who they assessed as being change agents. In recognition of this, these individuals were then awarded certificates carrying the names and logos of all participating organisations.

Clearly, this vision was novel in its approach to the development of competencies. One team member described the way in which member organisations, within the Learning Organisation Network, would work together in this process as a 'kind of change agent keiretsu'. It required the commitment of all concerned to the integrity of the process but since the essence of the change agent competencies is a recognition of continual individual and 'organisational' learning, this was in keeping with the aims and objectives of the Learning Organisation Network.

The process

Rather than start with a blank sheet of paper, the team at the Rover Learning Business carried out an initial trawl of existing development work in the area of change management, before they embarked on devising their own set of change agent competencies. They contacted several professional bodies but found that the competency work currently underway appeared to be developed by 'systems professionals and lawyers who had little feeling for people'.

As a result, over a three-month period, the Rover Learning Business started work on its own set of change agent competencies for leaders within the Rover organisation, which were linked closely to supporting the company's business strategy. The key question addressed by this work was: 'What competencies do you need to make the learning process work from a learning business viewpoint? Initially, 82

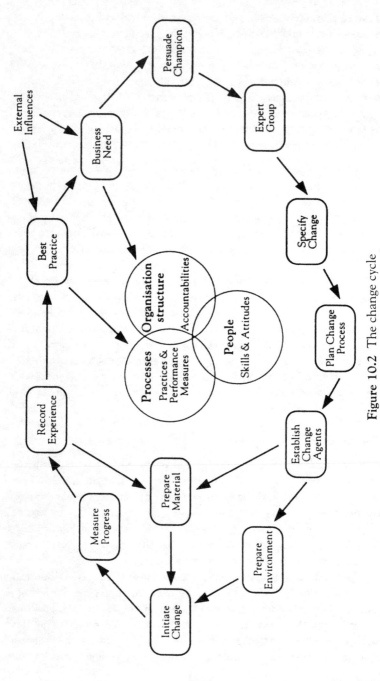

Figure 10.2 The change cycle

competencies were developed in this way and tested internally with change agents within Rover.

In networking with other organisations interested in developments in this area, Rover came across the work of Peritas, the ICL company specialising in people and organisational development. Peritas had developed a practical approach to competencies that it was marketing externally as a commercial enterprise. It was the initial contributions of both these organisations that the team from the Learning Organisation Network set to work on and Peritas has now used the Rover Framework to produce a model of change and change agent competencies for any business manager. The Learning Organisation Network is now validating these competencies in a variety of business environments.

The framework

The 'change cycle' in Figure 10.2 outlines the model of change within which Peritas has developed this set of change agent competencies.

The change cycle illustrates the stages that change agents have to go through in order to bring about value-adding change. Changing processes, organisational structure and the skills and attitudes of people, are in the three areas which are specifically identified as the targets of change.

Clearly, change agents have to understand the external influences that affect both **best practice** and their organisations' **business needs**. While many businesses will be affected by the same external influences, such as those which impact the economic environment generally, change agents will also be expected to appreciate factors that specifically impact their organisations.

From **best practice and business needs** the Learning Organisation Network team have developed a set of competencies for each of the areas identified in the change cycle.

The future

Although still in its infancy, the process by which these competencies have been developed so far has generated some considerable interest in Europe, where at a recent meeting of the European Consortium for Learning Organisations, the UK's work in this area was recognised as being significantly further advanced than that of its continental partners. A study group has now been set up in Finland to change and develop these competencies further.

Meanwhile, while recognising that those competencies are not cast in stone, organisations in the Learning Organisation Network are soon to be invited to make a more tangible commitment to the competencies developed so far, by offering the use of their corporate logos on the first certificates issued to those individuals recognised as competent change agents.

—— 11 ——

Making the Most of New Forms of Assessment

Within the new system of NVQs, assessment is a 'process of obtaining evidence and making judgements about that evidence'. More traditional forms of assessment require assessors both to determine the standards to be achieved and to assess evidence against those standards (as in a course-based programme of study). Within NVQs, the standards are already established and are in explicit (and written) format for both assessor and assessee. Assessment decisions therefore focus on whether the assessee has presented sufficient evidence of the right quality.

11.1 EVIDENCE OF COMPETENCE

Assessment of normal work performance offers the most natural form of evidence of competence. Where this is not possible, perhaps due to operational constraints or requirements of health and safety, workplace assessment can be supplemented by simulations, or by competency tests (like skills tests). In general, most observation of workplace assessment will need to be supplemented by at least oral questioning in order to determine evidence of transferability of skills and knowledge application across the specified range of work activity.

Evidence of performance can also be obtained during the course of a training programme when trainees practise and demonstrate skills and application of knowledge. In this way, assessment can be integrated with the learning process and provide useful feedback to trainees.

Given this performance-focused nature of new forms of assessment, how best can they be used to benefit your company?

11.2 PERFORMANCE APPRAISAL AND MANPOWER PLANNING

The previous chapter briefly outlined the use of competence-based standards within performance appraisal systems, and suggested that ongoing assessment may be treated as formative and thus contribute to the annual performance appraisal. It is worth noting again here, though, that you should avoid making the annual performance appraisal a 'summative' assessment which leads directly to the award of an NVQ. This would reinstate a time-based element to the achievement of NVQs, whereas one of their key benefits is individual access to awards based on individual performance.

Ongoing assessment, using competence-based systems, provides an up-to-date audit of individual and group performance. You might want to consider the best ways in which you can collate information to maintain your own records of improved performance.

As individuals are assessed, and achieve units of competence, you may wish to record this centrally to contribute to your manpower planning activities. This is also particularly relevant where you need to draw together project teams for particular assignments. You might consider the use of computerised systems for recording current skill levels; there are a variety available or under development which can be used for this purpose.

11.3 ASSESSMENT AND TRAINING

The design and delivery of training, using competence-based standards and assessment, is perhaps one of the most attractive benefits to individual companies (see Fletcher 1997a).

However, the issue of assessment in relation to training needs analysis and evaluation is also a key contributor to improvement of company performance.

11.4 TRAINING NEEDS ANALYSIS

Using explicit standards of performance, assessment of current levels of skill and knowledge, and identification of the 'training gap' are greatly facilitated. This process also ensures a common standard both for the initial assessment process, and for the targeted training which follows.

Trainers will need to be experienced in the use of competence-based standards and in their assessment. Line managers, if trained in work-based assessment, will be in an ideal position to identify training needs of both individuals and groups and pass this information on to the training department.

This somewhat changes the role of the trainer, but in line with current trends. The trainer becomes a key adviser and consultant in the company and provides support to line managers in both the needs-analysis and solution-finding role.

11.5 INDIVIDUAL DEVELOPMENT PLANS

The introduction and use of individual development plans are worth consideration. As competence-based assessment is *individualised*, linking assessment to personal and career development becomes a simpler process to operate within the company.

Again, you will need to consider the supporting structure of development plans and career progression. You may need to modify your existing in-company schemes, particularly in the context of documentation and recording systems. You might also like to consider ways in which *self-assessment* can be incorporated into the ongoing development process.

Information from individual development plans could be collated to contribute to annual training strategies and detailed plans.

11.6 MEETING NVQ CRITERIA

Whether you use documentation and procedures available within the relevant NVQ structure, or you choose to devise your own, a key requirement is that the assessment scheme meets the criteria set by the NCVQ.

The NVQ criteria relate to *quality of assessment* and *maintenance of national standards*. They also ensure that an *equal opportunities policy* is incorporated into working practice.

If you operate an in-company assessment scheme, you may want to link the development of your employees to in-company training programmes. This is acceptable as long as your in-company specifications for achievement of NVQs do not make completion of these training programmes mandatory.

DERBY COLLEGE : WILMORTON
LIBRARY

Individuals may learn in a variety of ways, including through work experience. NVQs are awarded for *successful assessment of competence performance*, not for attendance on specified courses.

11.7 GETTING HELP

If you are considering ways in which you can make the best use of competence-based assessment, there are a number of sources of information and direct support.

Awarding bodies

These bodies will be able to provide information regarding assessment requirements for particular NVQs, and for APL. They also provide external verifiers and can advise you of the fees involved. Remember, some ILBs are also awarding bodies.

Colleges

Many colleges have now radically changed their provision and some operate as approved assessment centres. Check with your local college provider to see what services are available. These may include college assessors who can visit the company, APL, or assistance with development programmes. Make sure the college has trained assessors and the facilities to assess in relevant occupational areas.

Private providers (approved NVQ Centres)

Some private training providers will be recommended by ILBs or approved by TECs and can help you with the development of standards, introduction of competence-based assessment, APL, assessor training and so on. Make sure you choose a provider who has experience in the field of competence-based provision.

Accredited Training Centres

The majority of these centres, which offer training in relation to national training programmes (eg, training credits and ET) are based in colleges. Their provision has recently expanded to include a more diverse range of training programmes. They can also assist with assessor training.

Whichever type of assistance you choose, it is best first to consider exactly what type of help you need within all areas of competence-based provision. It is usually advantageous to use a single source which can provide help across the board than to find you have to contract with two or three different organisations to achieve your total objectives.

Assessor/Verifier Awards

In 1993, national standards for assessors and verifiers were published (to be revised in 1997/8). In addition, the publication of the Common Accord confirmed the requirement for accredited staff in NVQ centres (including employer premises). The following section provides information on the Assessor and Verifier Awards and how to achieve them, and on the Common Accord.

INFORMATION SECTION

Assessor and Verifier Awards

In 1993, the Training and Development Lead Body (TDLB) approved units of competence for assessors and verifiers who operate within the NVQ system. These units received NCVQ approval and were launched for use by all assessors and verifiers.

In addition the Common Accord was published in the same year. This document confirmed that all assessors and verifiers for NVQs would be required to achieve the TDLB units (currently within 12 months of registration).

The assessor and verifier units cover all roles involved in NVQ operation:

- Unit D31 – designing assessment
- Unit D32 – workplace assessor
- Unit D33 – assessing diverse evidence (eg, portfolios, APL)
- Unit D34 – internal verifier
- Unit D35 – external verifier
- Unit D36 – APL adviser.

In line with NCVQ requirements, these units are achieved by **demonstration of competence in the role**. Thus, all assessors and verifiers must actually undertake the role in order to provide sufficient valid evidence of performance.

This creates something of a 'chicken and egg' situation for many people – you need the assessor awards to be accredited (or licensed in some cases), but you need to assess people in order to achieve the award!

The Common Accord document acknowledges this dilemma and arrangements now include a period of 12 months in which all practising assessors and verifiers can collect sufficient evidence for accreditation. During this time, their work will be monitored by an approved verifier.

The quality assurance system for NVQs (in ideal form) operates as follows:

- External verifier (employee of awarding body)
- Internal verifier (in-house at assessment centre, which can be an employer)
- Work place assessors (in-house at assessment centre)
- Candidates.

Employers can become approved centres for NVQs (although this is not always practical or cost-effective for all NVQs or all companies). To do so, the employer must demonstrate that the above quality assurance framework can operate in-house, that assessors and verifiers are working towards accredited status and that the in-house assessment system meets national requirements.

This can get a bit unwieldy when a number of NVQs are being introduced, especially if each has its own assessment documentation and each is given by a different awarding body! For this reason, many companies make use of national standards (including those for assessors and verifiers) without introducing NVQs. However, by designing an in-house assessment system to cover all relevant occupational areas, a company can overcome these difficulties.

In-house assessors and verifiers must be trained (see p. 85 for help in this area) – it is dangerous to assume that the use of a competence-based system can simply be 'picked up': it requires an adjustment in thinking. A lack of adequate training can result in a poor quality operation – which will add nothing to the organisational or individual benefits of introduction.

Further information on the assessor and verifier awards can be obtained from the awarding bodies. Each awarding body has its own development and accreditation system (and related costs). Costs should include:

- individual registration fee (check if this covers all units or only one)
- certification fee (per unit)

■ licence fee (not applicable to all awarding bodies).

Check also whether the registration fee includes provision of materials for use by assessors – and whether these are mandatory (they should not be)!

The awarding bodies also approve centres to offer the assessor and verifier awards. This will include provision of training, assessment and recommendation for certification. Check carefully on costs involved which could include:

■ training of assessors/verifiers
■ adviser support
■ work place assessment
■ telephone support
■ portfolio assessment (not mandatory, observation is better quality)
■ individual interview following portfolio assessment
■ recommendation for certification
■ awarding body registration fee
■ awarding body materials
■ certification fee.

Make sure you get value for money as well as quality of delivery and support!

You can obtain full lists of approved centres from the awarding bodies.

There are also various open learning programmes on the market and an assessor development pack is available from NCVQ.

Remember – assessors do *not* achieve their 'D' Units by attending a training programme. They must demonstrate competence like any other NVQ candidate.

The Common Accord

During 1992, officers of the National Council for Vocational Qualifications (NCVQ) worked with the main UK awarding bodies to develop the content of the Common Accord (revised 1997).

The Common Accord principles are intended to enhance the quality and cost-effectiveness of NVQ assessment and verification processes operated by awarding bodies.

The Accord also aims to emphasise the coherence of the NVQ framework making it easier for users to understand NVQs.

The main features of the Accord are:

- **common terminology** to describe the roles of the individuals and organisations in the assessment and quality assurance system
- **certification to national standards** for assessors and verifiers
- **defined roles in quality assurance** for both awarding bodies and the organisations which they approve to offer NVQs
- **explicit criteria** for approving organisations to offer NVQs
- **quality assurance and control systems** to ensure rigour and monitor equal opportunities implementation.

The Common Accord document was circulated for consultation at the end of 1992 and the published document reports that this 'generated support in terms of both its concept and content with the overwhelming majority of respondents agreeing the basic principles. Almost all respondents were in favour of the increased quality expected as a result of the accord' (NCVQ 1993).

Perhaps one of the most interesting aspects of the document is the recognition by national bodies of 'the importance of reinforcing the concept of flexibility within the main principles of the Accord.' The document refers to the need for awarding bodies to have a 'sensible degree' of discretion to adapt elements of the Accord to circumstances.

To be more explicit, the document goes on to state that this may refer particularly to the frequency and duration of external verification visits and the length of time for which an external verifier is appointed.

There are many, perhaps, who would say that this degree of flexibility is inadequate. A number of difficulties experienced in implementation of NVQs go beyond those created by the frequency and duration of external verifier visits; they include difficulties with operating the **structure** of the NVQ, and with **interpretation** of the standards. Even more so, difficulties in **operationalising assessment practice**, particularly within a small company setting, are on the increase as the NVQ implementation rolls out.

Further difficulties appear to be created by the direct link to National Education and Training Targets (NETTs). The TECs are supporting the NVQ implementation (with financial as well as practical support), but they too have targets to meet. These targets are quantitative – numbers of people achieving certification within a given timescale. Such quantitative targets do little to aid the **overall quality** which the Common Accord goes some way to help achieve.

However, it must also be recognised that the Common Accord is a step in the right direction to help deal with complaints of confusion and bureaucracy within the NVQ framework. Unless a common operational structure with common quality requirements and common terminology is established, it is unlikely that the NVQ system will be taken up by industry to the extent required by the National Targets.

DETAILS OF THE COMMON ACCORD

In outline, the Common Accord aims to provide:

Common Terminology:

The standard terms for the main functions and roles in the assessment and verification system are presented in the Common Accord as follows:

- **assessment** is carried out by an **assessor**
- **internal verification** is carried out by an **internal verifier**
- **external verification** is carried out by an **external verifier**
- **approved centre** – is approved by an awarding body to offer NVQ assessment. Each approved centre must have, or have access to, an appropriately qualified internal verifier.

In the case of a small centre (such as a small business), it is acceptable for the external verifier to carry out the functions of internal verification. It is not acceptable, however, to combine the functions of assessment and verification for the same assessment decision.

An approved centre is not necessarily a single site. Any company, for example, can become an approved centre; it is the organisation which is approved. A central site could operate a number of 'satellite' centres – which may be regional offices or operational units.

Conditional approval is not to be used as a mechanism within the quality assurance system. A centre must demonstrate how initial development leads to their meeting full approval criteria.

CERTIFICATION TO NATIONAL STANDARDS FOR ASSESSORS AND VERIFIERS

Following the launch of national standards for assessors and verifiers, which were developed by the Training and Development Lead Body (TDLB), the use of these standards was incorporated into quality assurance requirements for operational NVQ approved centres.

It is now a requirement that assessors and verifiers should establish their competence by holding certificates of unit credit in relevant national units. These targets for unit certification were agreed, and published in the Common Accord, as follows:

Assessors	Unit D32 and/or D33
Internal verifiers	Unit **D34,** D32 and D33
External verifiers	Unit **D35**, D32 and D33.

The published requirement recognised that these targets were not immediately achievable and therefore stated that **by 1995** (April), external and internal verifiers were to be qualified with the single unit indicated in bold type above.

Also by April 1995, approval arrangements for centres required that the centre had an action plan to certificate all existing and new assessors within an agreed timescale. From April 1995 onwards, all assessment decisions by assessors who are still working towards certification should normally be supported by an assessor or verifier who has gained certification.

The assessor and verifier units are available from all major awarding bodies. Each awarding body will have a full list of centres which are approved to provide development and assessment for assessors.

OCCUPATIONAL BACKGROUND OF ASSESSORS AND INTERNAL VERIFIERS

There has been much debate about the need for assessors and internal verifiers to be 'competent' in the occupational area for which they assess. NCVQ Guidance, published in the Common Accord, is as follows:

Assessors, internal and external verifiers will all need some background which will enable them to judge whether a candidate's performance is meeting the specified standards of occupational competence. It is evident from the diversity of views expressed through consultation that the precise background that would be appropriate will vary between sectors and roles. A standard requirement for occupational background would thus be inappropriate. Instead, for each award, the awarding body should specify the occupational competence or experience considered necessary to perform each role. (Common Accord, NCVQ 1993, p. 5)

Note that the phrase 'competence or experience' is used. A requirement for 'competence' would imply that any assessor would need to hold the relevant NVQ in order to assess in any particular occupational area.

DEFINED ROLES IN QUALITY ASSURANCE

The Common Accord defines these roles as follows:

Approved centres

An approved centre takes charge of delivering assessment for (one or more designated) NVQs on a day-to-day basis. The centre should have effective internal procedures to ensure the quality and consistency of assessment. Centres are responsible for providing sufficient competent assessors and internal verifiers.

In the case of small centres, the individual who performs the internal verification function may come from another organisation – thus allowing for consortia arrangements.

Awarding bodies

Awarding bodies are responsible for verifying that assessment in an approved centre is carried out systematically, validly and to national standards. External verifiers are appointed by, and employees of, awarding bodies. The awarding body will also have an appeals procedure to deal with instances where a centre wishes to dispute approval decisions.

External verifiers

External verifiers check the internal systems of the approved centres and also sample assessment practices and decisions. An external verifier also provides support and advice to centres and has the authority to recommend withdrawal of approval when circumstances merit this.

Explicit criteria for approving centres

Common criteria for approval of centres, agreed by all awarding bodies and published in the Common Accord, relate to the following areas:

- management systems
- physical resources
- staff resources

- assessment
- quality assurance and control
- equal opportunities.

Each awarding body provides full details on its application for approval and the initial visit by the external verifier will help centres plan to meet all the specified criteria. All centres must be able to provide evidence, through action planning, that criteria can, indeed, be met. In the absence of such evidence approval will not be granted.

Full NVQs vs Units

The Common Accord contains recognition of the situation in which some centres will not feel able to offer a full NVQ but should not be excluded from the approval process. It is a requirement of the Common Accord, therefore, that procedures are in place to allow centres to be approved to offer NVQ units.

Adding further NVQs to approved centre operations

A centre which is already approved to offer a particular NVQ may wish to add further NVQs (or units). In this instance, guidance is as follows:

(a) where the occupational area, individuals involved as internal verifiers, and quality assurance systems are the same, then a simple application in writing may be appropriate
(b) where the quality assurance systems are the same as for an existing approval, but the NVQ is in a different area, then the awarding body may use abbreviated approval processes, carrying forward the appraisal made previously against certain approved criteria.

Duration of approval

Centre approval should be for a fixed period, taking account of the period of NCVQ accreditation for the award. External verifiers should also be appointed to centres for a fixed period.

Centre approval and verification criteria

A full set of criteria can be found in the Common Accord; the following provides a summary.

1. Management systems
   The centre must specify and maintain an effective system for managing NVQs.

2. Administrative arrangements
   Accurate records of the assessment of candidates must be maintained and awarding body administrative requirements fulfilled.
3. Physical resources
   Sufficient resources must be available to assess candidates for NVQs.
4. Staff resources
   Staff resources must be sufficient to deliver assessment for NVQs.
5. Assessment
   A system for valid and reliable assessment to national standards must be specified and maintained.
6. Quality assurance and control
   An effective system for quality assurance and control must be maintained.
7. Equal opportunities and access
   There must be a clear commitment to equal opportunities.

(Common Accord, NCVQ 1993)

COSTS OF OPERATING NVQs

Costs for operating particular NVQs vary quite widely. The Common Accord gives no guidelines in this respect. However, in an attempt to provide some guidance, the following checklist will help you to ensure that you have considered all relevant aspects of implementation, including operating as an NVQ centre.

Centre approval costs:

Initial registration/approval fees
Most awarding bodies will charge an approval fee. This will cover the cost of visits by the external verifier during the first year, and may also cover the cost of issue of relevant materials (although this is an additional cost in some cases). Registration fees may vary from £150 to £1500 and are usually payable annually to relevant awarding bodies.

Candidate registration fees
There is usually a requirement to register individual candidates. This includes the cost of administration for entering the candidate details on the awarding body database and issue of registration documents (these

can be a single form, or a log book). Costs again vary from around £20 to £150 per candidate. Check if this cost includes certification and the NCVQ levy.

Candidate log books/assessment packs

Issue of candidate materials may be included in the candidate registration fee (see above), but you need to ensure that you clarify this. For some awards, issue of awarding body log books and/or assessment packs is optional, for others it is mandatory. Candidate packs for the assessor awards are issued by (for example) City & Guilds at £5 each.

Costs of assessment

You will need to consider the costs of assessment carefully. If you become an approved centre, your in-house assessors will need training and development; they too will need to be assessed against the national standards for assessors. Introducing competence-based assessment as an integral part of performance management takes time, and those undertaking the assessment and verification roles will need time to familiarise themselves with the new system and incorporate it into their everyday activity. The assessment process should, eventually, become a full part of performance management, but should not add huge additional workloads.

If you do not become an NVQ Centre then you will need to consider how, where and what form of external assessment support you need to buy in. Check with the awarding bodies for approved centres and get quotes from several before deciding.

Financial support for the assessment process is available from TECs through the Skill Choice initiative. Contact your local TEC for more information.

Certification costs

Both unit and full NVQ certification are available. A full NVQ certificate can cost between £20 and £150. Awarding bodies calculate costs of verification and certification on the basis of the number of people who are likely to pass through the assessment and certification process in a given year. As commercial organisations, they too have to recover their costs. (It is important therefore that the development stage of NVQs bears this in mind and keeps administration to a minimum.)

GNVQs

Guidance in respect of GNVQs, which are currently only offered by BTEC, City & Guilds and RSA, is published separately and available from NCVQ.

Part IV

Help Menu:
Quick Reference Guide
Glossary of Terms
Who to Contact
Funding Support

DERBY COLLEGE : WILMORTON
LIBRARY

Quick Reference Guide

Glossary of Terms

Accreditation   Formal recognition that individuals have shown evidence of performance which meets specified standards.

Assessment (competence-based)   Collection of evidence of performance by a variety of methods.

Awarding body   An examining or validating body. In a competence-based system, an awarding body has central responsibility for the quality, but not the methods of assessment.

Awards   A general term for qualifications issued by examining or validating bodies, ie, certificates, diplomas, etc.

Competence   The ability to perform a particular activity to a prescribed standard. Competence is a wide concept which embodies the ability to transfer skills and knowledge to new situations within the occupational area. It encompasses organisation and planning of work, innovation and coping with non-routine activities. It includes those qualities of personal effectiveness that are required in the workplace to deal with co-workers, managers and customers.

Continuous assessment   Assessment of competence on every occasion it is required during normal workplace activity. Used for formative assessment and to arrive at a cumulative judgement for final assessment purposes.

Credit accumulation   A system by which individuals can accumulate units of competence. When a specified combination of units has been achieved the individual can obtain a full NVQ.

Credit transfer   The use of an award (or credits towards one) as credit towards another award.

Element of competence   The descriptors of the activities necessary for the completion of the function described in a unit of competence.

Formative assessment   Assessment during a course, or over a period of workplace activity, which collects evidence of performance.

Industry Lead Body   An organisation comprised of industry education and trade union representatives with formal responsibility for the development of national standards of occupational competence and a framework of National Vocational Qualifications.

Moderation   A process or procedure to align standards of assessment between different test papers, different testing occasions, different examiners, different centres, etc.

National Vocational Qualification   A statement of competence defined by industry and based on nationally agreed standards of occupational competence.

Norm-referenced assessment   Assessment of an individual's ability in order to determine how well it compares with other individuals' abilities.

Occupational Standards Council (OSC)   A group of Industry Lead Bodies responsible for management of cross-industry standards and NVQs.

Performance criteria   Descriptors of required outcomes of workplace activities.

Range statements   Descriptors of the limits within which performance to the identified standard is expected if an individual is to be deemed competent. Range describes competent workplace performance, not the situations in which performance must be observed for assessment purposes.

Underpinning skills and knowledge   Identifies the knowledge and skill necessary to perform to the standards identified by the performance criteria in the contexts identified in the range statement.

Unit of competence   A descriptor of a discrete function carried out by an individual within an occupational area.

Who to Contact

What NVQs are available?	Regular NCVQ update *Monitor* from NCVQ 222 Euston Road London NW1 2BZ Relevant Industry Lead Body
What standards are available?	Relevant Industry Lead Body (ILB)
What standards are under development (if no ILB)?	Department for Education and Employment (DfEE) Moorfoot Sheffield S1 4PQ
How do you get access to the NCVQ database?	NCVQ 222 Euston Road London NW1 2BZ
How do you get in-company training recognised for credit exemption/advanced standing?	Your local college

What about qualifications in Scotland (SVQs)?	Scotvec Hanover House Douglas St Glasgow G2 7NQ

Funding Support – What is Available?

As more NVQs are developed and the implementation increases, so levels and types of funding available to support implementation are generated.

The main source of information regarding funding should be your local TEC (LECs in Scotland).

Help is available under a number of headings, these include:

Investors in People
Business Change
Business Development
Competence Audits/NVQ Service
Modern Apprenticeships
Skills for Small Business
Training for Work.

The Skill Choice initiative will probably be the best source of funding in respect of NVQ implementation for employers, providing a percentage of costs in respect of action planning (guidance), assessment planning and accreditation.

For Investors in People the TECs provide approved consultants to help with action planning and to undertake the assessment.

Business Change provides support with actions for change within the organisation.

TECs hold registers of approved consultants and providers. There is a regional and national register known as TECAssure. This will include the names of all approved individual consultants (they have to pay a fee for the approval process).

Some TECs also pay full fees for one of their approved consultants to undertake a 'competence audit' and 'action plan' – this will produce a detailed plan with costings for the introduction of NVQs in the most cost-effective and productive way. This is a worthwhile service which can save a great deal of time and money in the long run.

References

Beaumont, G (1996) *Review of Top 100 NVQs*, NCVQ, London.

BTEC (1990) *APL: General Guidelines*, Business and Technology Education Council: London.

CGLI (1988) *Assessment and Validation Procedures for APL*, City and Guilds: London.

C&G (1990) *Guidelines on Accreditation of Prior Learning*, City and Guilds: London.

CNAA (1984) *Access to Higher Education. Non-standards entry to CNAA first degree and Dip HE courses*, Council for National Academic Awards: London.

Coopers and Lybrand (1985) *A Challenge to Complacency; Changing Attitudes to Training*, Manpower Services Commission/National Economic Development Commission: Sheffield.

Employment Dept (1990) *Training and Enterprise Councils; A Prospectus for the 1990s*.

Employment Dept (1991) *Development of Assessable Standards for National Certification*, Standards/Methodology Unit (edited by Edward Fennell) HMSO: London.

Employment Dept (1993) *TECS 1992*.

Fletcher, S (1993) *Quality and Competence*, Kogan Page: London.

Fletcher, S (1997a) *Competence-Based Assessment Techniques*, 2nd edition, Kogan Page: London.

Fletcher, S (1997b) *Designing Competence-Based Training*, 2nd edition, Kogan Page: London.

Fletcher, S (1997c) *NVQ Assessment: A Handbook for the Paperless Portfolio*, Kogan Page: London.

HMSO (1988) *Employment for the 1990s*, HMSO: London.

HMSO (1986) *Working Together, Education and Training*, Government

White Paper Cmnd 9823, Department of Employment, HMSO: London.

Mansfield, B and Mathews, D (1985) *Job Competence: A Description for Use in Vocational Education and Training*, FESC/ESF Core Skills Project: Bristol.

MSC (1981) *A New Training Initiative: Agenda for Action*, Manpower Services Commission: Sheffield.

MSC/NEDC (1981) *A New Training Initiative: Agenda for Action*, HMSO: London.

MSC/NEDC (1986) *Review of Vocational Qualifications in England and Wales*.

NCVQ (1988a) *The NVQ Criteria and Related Guidance*, NCVQ: London.

NCVQ (1988b) *NVQs – What They Mean for You – A Guide*.

NCVQ (1988c) *Draft Corporate Plan 1988/9 – 1991/2*, NCVQ: London.

NCVQ (1989) 'Occupational standards for dental surgery assistants', *NCVQ R&D Report*, 1, December.

NCVQ (1993) *The Common Accord*, Employment Department: Sheffield (revised 1997).

NCVQ (1997) *Assessment for NVQs*, NCVQ: London.

NCVQ (quarterly) *NVQ Monitor*, NCVQ: London.

NEDC/MSC (1984) *Competence and Competition: Training and Education in the Federal Republic of Germany, The United States and Japan*, National Economic Development Office and Manpower Services Commission: Sheffield.

Randell, G (1984) *Staff Appraisal*, 3rd edition, Institute of Personnel Management: London.

Scotvec (1988) *The National Certificate. A Guide to Assessment*, Scotvec: Glasgow.

TDLB (1992) *National Standards for Training and Development*, Training and Development Lead Body/DfEE: London.

Training Agency (1988/90) *Competence and Assessment*, Standards Methodology Unit, Moorfoot, Sheffield.

Training Agency (1988/89) *Technical Guidance Notes*, Moorfoot, Sheffield.

Training Agency (1989) *Training and Enterprise, Priorities for Action 1990/91*.

Index